Architecture + Animation

Guest-edited by Bob Fear

ΔD   Architectural Design +

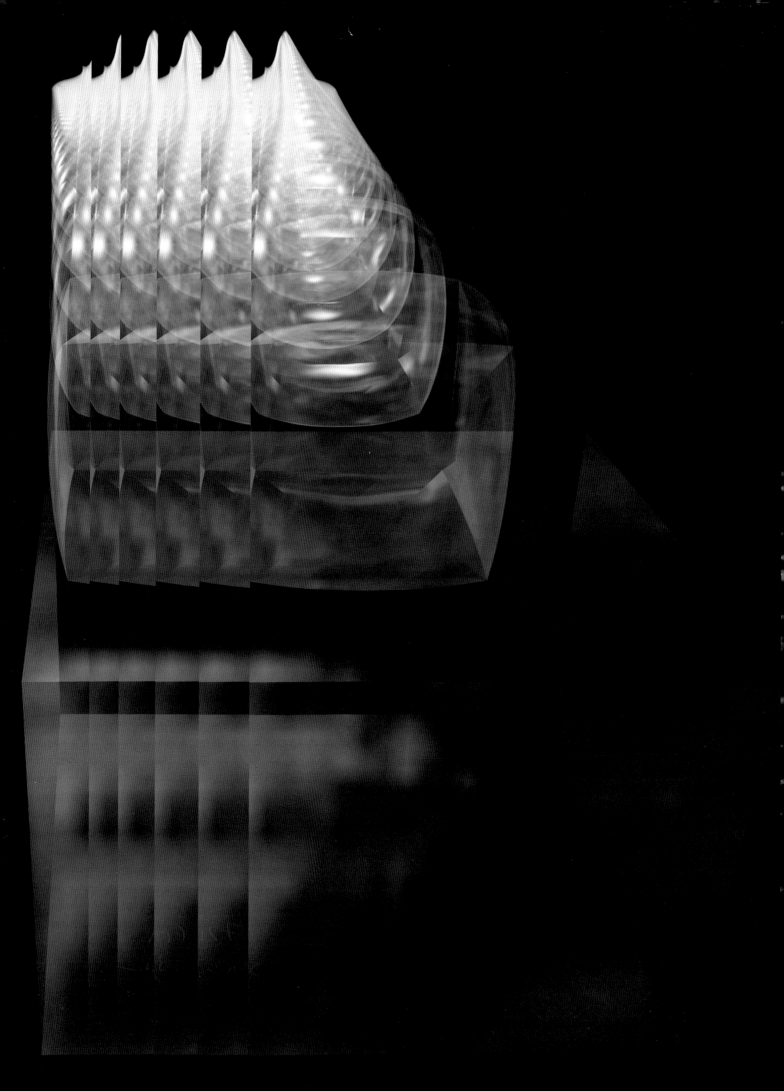

ΔD Architectural Design

Architecture + Animation

Guest-edited by Bob Fear

WILEY-ACADEMY

AD

Architectural Design
Vol 71 No 2 April 2001

ISBN 0-471-49629-4
Profile No 150

Editorial Offices
International House
Ealing Broadway Centre
London W5 5DB
T: +44 (0)20 8326 3800
F: +44 (0)20 8326 3801
E: info@wiley.co.uk

Editor
Maggie Toy

Executive Editor
Helen Castle

Production
Mariangela Palazzi-Williams
Famida Rasheed

Art Director
Christian Küsters ↳ CHK Design

Design Assistant
Owen Peyton Jones ↳ CHK Design

Advertisement Sales
01243 843272

Photo Credits
AD Architectural Design

Abbreviated positions
b=bottom, c=centre, l=left, r=right, t=top

Cover image: © Gregory More.

p 4 and pp 6–16 © Mark Burry, Grant Dunlop and Simon Anson; pp 17–19 © Bernard Tschumi; pp 20–7 © Gregory More; pp 28–35 © Ali Rahim; pp 36–9 © Oosterhuis.nl; pp 40–8 © Chris Romero; pp 49–52 © Timothy Craig Durfee; pp 53–55 © SCI-Arc; pp 56–63 © dECOI Architects; pp 64–5 © Pia Ednie-Brown; pp 67–9 © Tom Kovac; pp 70--3 © Jessica Lynch, pp 74–80 © Greg Lynn FORM; pp 83–5 © Neil Spiller/photos of sketchbook by Chris Bigg@V23; pp 86–91 © Ben Nicholson, the LOAF House Building was created by Peter Ippolito.

AD+
P 95+ all courtesy and © Monica Pidgeon, except the portrait of Tony Towndrow is by LaFayette, London 1939 (courtesy Monica Pidgeon); pp 101–8 © P Karle/R Buxbaum Freie Architekten; p 111 courtesy Agenzia Spaziale Italiana.

Subscription Offices UK
John Wiley & Sons Ltd.
Journals Administration Department
1 Oldlands Way, Bognor Regis
West Sussex, PO22 9SA
T: +44 (0)1243 843272
F: +44 (0)1243 843232
E: cs-journals@wiley.co.uk

Subscription Offices USA and Canada
John Wiley & Sons Ltd.
Journals Administration Department
605 Third Avenue
New York, NY 10158
T: +1 212 850 6645
F: +1 212 850 6021
E: subinfo@wiley.com

Annual Subscription Rates 2001
Institutional Rate: UK £150
Personal Rate: UK £97
Student Rate: UK £70
Institutional Rate: US $225
Personal Rate: US $145
Student Rate: US $105

AD is published bi-monthly.
Prices are for six issues and include postage and handling charges. Periodicals postage paid at Jamaica, NY 11431. Air freight and mailing in the USA by Publications Expediting Services Inc, 200 Meacham Avenue, Eimont, NY 11003

Single Issues UK: £19.99
Single Issues outside UK: US $32.50
Order two or more titles and postage is free. For orders of one title ad £2.00/US $5.00. To receive order by air please add £5.50/US $10.00

Postmaster
Send address changes to *AD* c/o Expediting Services Inc, 200 Meacham Avenue, Long Island, NY 11003

Printed in Italy. All prices are subject to change without notice.
[ISSN: 0003-8504]

Cover images by Gregory More.

The relationship between architecture and animation is ripe for scrutiny. Over the last decade, animation has emerged in architectural practice as a sophisticated design toy. Initially, at least, animatory techniques have been able to impress almost on the strength of their novelty alone. This is true of their use in filmic walkthroughs, as popular presentational gimmicks, and in the adoption in the creative process where they have been responsible for alluring, futuristic images, gyrating through space. In this issue of *Architectural Design*, animation's place in architecture comes of age. The blind infatuation of the early years is at a close. We are entering a challenging new era, as the relationship is being stretched and tested in every way. Mark Burry in his Our World project at RMIT, in Melbourne, and Tim Durfee and Terry Surjan teaching at SCI-Arc, in Los Angeles, for instance, are using animatory techniques in their studios as a means to question architectural and spatial perceptions. A by-product of the introduction of animation has been the folding of time into the creative process. Two contributors, Gregory More and Ali Rahim, tackle this new preoccupation from very different angles. More traces the introduction of time into the medium through the work of early 20th-century animators, while Rahim explores how the use of animation techniques in the creative process might optimise on unpredictable, irreversible and qualitative manner time, as formulated by Henri Bergson. Architects' experimentation with animation and other digital techniques has helped to erode the boundaries between different media, if not separate disciplines: Bernard Tschumi uses animation to communicate, virtually, the experiential qualities of one of his own completed buildings, Lerner Hall; Chris Romero constructs hybrid constructions, which integrate computational and physical environments with a range of media components, in order to create installations for public participation; and Tim Durfee employs his architectural knowledge and spatial skills to create an informational infrastructure for a CD-ROM magazine. Far beyond the surface excitement of the last ten years, architects are also realising the more profound potential of animated architecture. For Nicholson, it is life itself — the essence, the smile and the flicker across the face. Kas Oosterhuis turns the tables and as technology runs wild, he foresees a time in which digital technology invades the building and becomes the moving object, rendering humans no more than software. Mark Goulthorpe of dECOi and Pia Ednie-Brown, in very different ways, acknowledge animation's emergence as a cultural phenomenon. For Neil Spiller, the evangelist of cyberspace and proselytiser of new technologies, though the honeymoon period is over. As a testament to the absorption of animation into architecture, he calls for its more discerning and questioning use.⚁ *Helen Castle*

Opposite
Mark Burry, 'Our World' project.

5

Beyond Animation

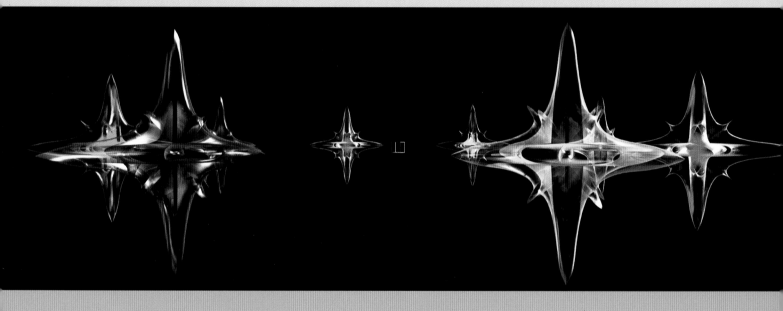

Animation techniques are most commonly employed by architects
to create cinematic 'walk-throughs' or as a generative design tool.
In his work at Deakin University, Australia, Mark Burry is taking
their application beyond architecture. Pertinently, he is employing
animation — a term which by its very definition refers to 'life' —
to pursue philosophical preoccupations centring on pre- and
postexistence. Through the Our World project, he is further testing
the restrictions of animation and spatial representation of the
third dimension.

For a discussion of architectural space and time, let us take 'to animate' as meaning to give life, and 'animation' as the condition of being animated. Respectively, their antonyms shall be 'to take life away' and 'being inanimate'. It is difficult enough for most mortals to comprehend the darker implications of the states of being quick and being dead with complete psychological comfort, still more so to comprehend being agent to these states in others. Dilemmas that have emanated from our difficulty in reaching a deeper understanding of existence, pre-existence and life after death encourage and support various streams of moral constructions and beliefs. Culturally and anthropologically there is ample evidence of our creative efforts to come to terms with the

an iterative design generation or as an evaluation procedure.

The first of these opportunities for architectural animation is a latter-day substitute and expansion of the perspectivist's craft, with the inclusion of the representation of movement around and through buildings. This is a relatively extreme process compared to traditional architectural exposé such as physical models that place absolute reliance on our cognitive and interpretative skills. It is a contemporary technological triumph that is often abused, not least for the misrepresentation of occupancy and its ignorance of the human state of being. Such client presentations can entail deliberately distorted renditions of space and time that do not necessarily possess genuine filmic qualities. Of course, in cases that do demonstrate such qualities, animation – with some allegiance to film

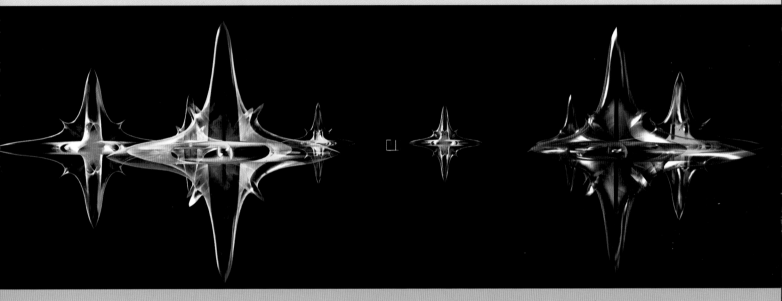

unknown world since we first began to think and to make as human beings.

Associating such ideas as the animate and inanimate to architecture can provide both profoundly philosophical and lyrically descriptive arguments for an apparently material substantiation of four-dimensional spatial moulding through the inclusion of time. The uses of animation in its variety of treatments therefore offer very modern possibilities for architectural thinking, depending on the depth of engagement and the motivation behind such use. In this regard there are at least two opportunities for animation to be used as part of the development and representation of ideas: firstly as architecture considered and represented through animated treatment of 'real buildings'; and secondly at a conceptual level where animation is used as a device in architectural design, most usually as part of

theory – might be regarded as 'art', and as a new and legitimate source of creative exposition.

The second state of animation referred to above is the representation of morphological shifts in architectural form through movement in reaction to, or in sympathy with, external forces or even ideologies. Often time is taken as the fourth dimension and is the device by which such shifts are explored.

My educational and professional interest is in using animation to go beyond ordinary spatial representation in order to look at the possibilities of using the new cinematic crafts with architectural ideation. This focus can seek voices for the deeper philosophical preoccupations that surround the conditions of pre- or postexistence. This may mean going beyond animation itself. Such voices benefit from narrative support and with this in mind we can do little better, I believe, than to draw upon Flann O'Brien's *The Third Policeman*[1] as a source to furnish elements of transubstantiation pertinent to a non-time-based multidimensional

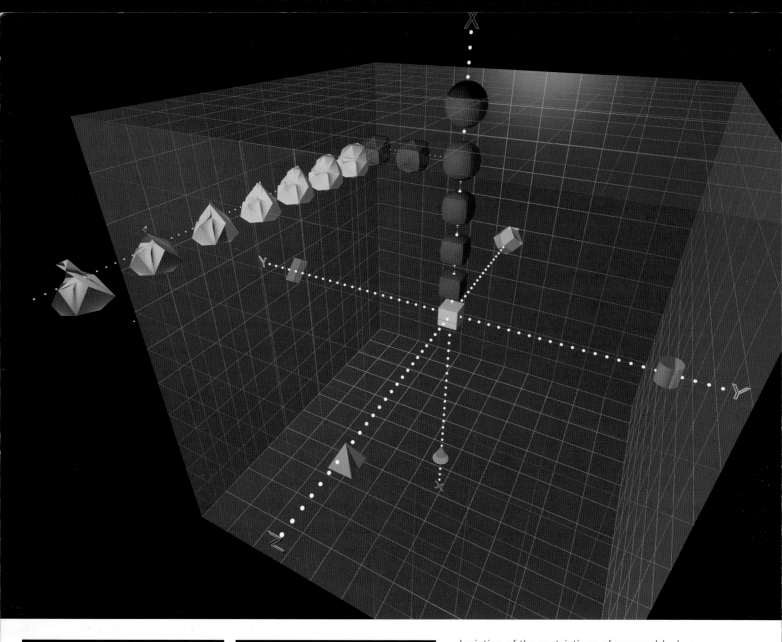

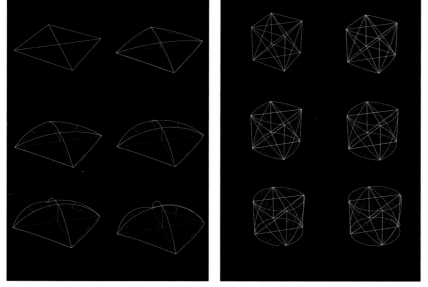

depiction of the restrictions of our world when constructed in Cartesian terms. In this discussion animation is used perversely to provide evidence of both the restrictions of our abilities to represent space beyond the third dimension and the limitations of animation itself.

The Third Policeman was written early during the Second World War in neutral Eire by the Irish writer Flann O'Brien, also known as Myles na Gopaleen (but whose real name was Brian O'Nolan). The book was not published, however, until 1967, a year after the author's death. My copy includes a note from the author:

> Joe had been explaining things in the meantime. He said it was again the beginning of the unfinished, the rediscovery of the familiar, the re-experience of the already suffered, the fresh forgetting of the unremembered. Hell goes round and round. In shape it is circular and by nature it is interminable, repetitive and very nearly unbearable.[2]

It is difficult to write about *The Third Policeman* without giving away details of the bizarre plot; the character 'Joe' shall remain obscure here to all who have not read the book .[3] In general terms it deals with the layering of spaces upon spaces, conflicting states of existence and linking moral dimensions to those that govern the physical realm. Most acutely, the novel deals with time

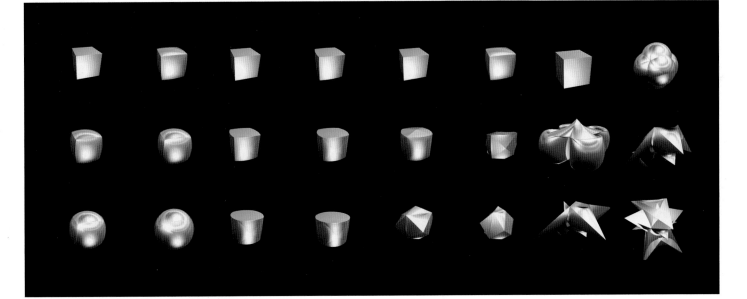

through time: the overlapping multiplicity and the endlessness of time as but one condition of eternity. At the same time and ineffably linked, the reader is treated to a regular discussion of the possible thinness of space and issues of scalability from a fundamentally anthropomorphic viewpoint. Such dilemmas are always represented in bizarre and darkly humorous contexts. The thinness of space, for example, is described by the (almost) two-dimensional police station that features prominently in the book. 'Atomic theory' would have us believe that an individual who makes heavy use of a bicycle will, in time, become part being, part machine in proportions that vary with the degree of exposure. The novel's protagonist, a sallow intellectual manqué (and murderer) draws heavily upon the thoughts of a fictitious philosopher named de Selby who, in turn, is substantially quoted throughout the book especially by the use of copious footnotes. Theories that determine that the world is not so much spherical as 'sausage shaped' are derived from de Selby's proposition that the four cardinal points of geography are in fact just two. North and south, apparently, are essentially the same given that circumnavigation in either direction has the same outcome. De Selby argues that were the east–west axis the equivalent of north–south there would be just one cardinal point; that there are two is evidence of a world not truly spherical in shape.

Early in the novel winds are identified not only by their cardinal origins but also by their colours, a skill claimed to have been lost to humankind in more recent times. Longevity is determined by the direction of the wind during birth, with the original birthday and subsequent ones marked by the addition of a new suit in the colour of the birth wind on each occasion. Each annually provided attire is worn over the previous garments. The suits are made from

diaphanous gossamer so filmy that they can only be seen by their edges when held to the light. As they numerically increase as a series they build up in colour and, when eventually combining to produce black, they herald the wearer's death day. Some colours are therefore less good than others. Pink, for example, tends towards purple and subsequently black in fewer years than, say, yellow, a luckier wind to have been born by. (See The eight birth winds... p7.)

The combination of the various episodes within the novel, absurd as they seem in isolation, are moralistic, not least in the evocation of the human lifespan as being but naught within the undisclosable totality of the space–time continuum. The novel appears as apparent nonsense until in the final pages the complexities of its space–time context are revealed in retrospectively chilling obviousness. Such fertile material thus provides a wealth of opportunity for an inspired exploration of visual narrative using contemporary animation techniques. Our World, the project described here, is not inspired specifically by the book, but it is nevertheless aligned to the central questions that it poses: definitions of time and space beyond the animate, espoused in the first line of the book where a fellow human being is rendered inanimate by the actions of the novel's principal protagonist.

Our World is a collaborative exercise in which we seek to look at aspects of hybridisation and the subsequent cataloguing of the experimental outcomes. To do so we need to be tidy and construct a scenario of linguistic commonality so that our individual iterative explorations can be amalgamated and collectivised. The task is essentially simple: to work towards a mutual understanding of the topologies of various Phileban forms (cubes, spheres, pyramids, etc) so that we can computationally adjust the spatial characteristics of their respective geographies in order to represent transitional states – the morphing of one form into another. This enterprise requires a context, and one way of organising the transitions so that all participants are clear about the route and outcomes is

Opposite top
A view of the general layout of 'Our World' showing the original Phileban forms and one three-dimensional trajectory of change.

Opposite bottom left
Cube-to-sphere surface definition diagrams.

Opposite bottom right
Cube-to-cylinder surface definition diagrams.

Above from the top
Normal cube-to-sphere surface metamorphosis.

Normal cube-to-cylinder surface metamorphosis.

Normal cube-to-polyhedra surface metamorphosis.

Abnormal (progeric) cube surface metamorphosis.

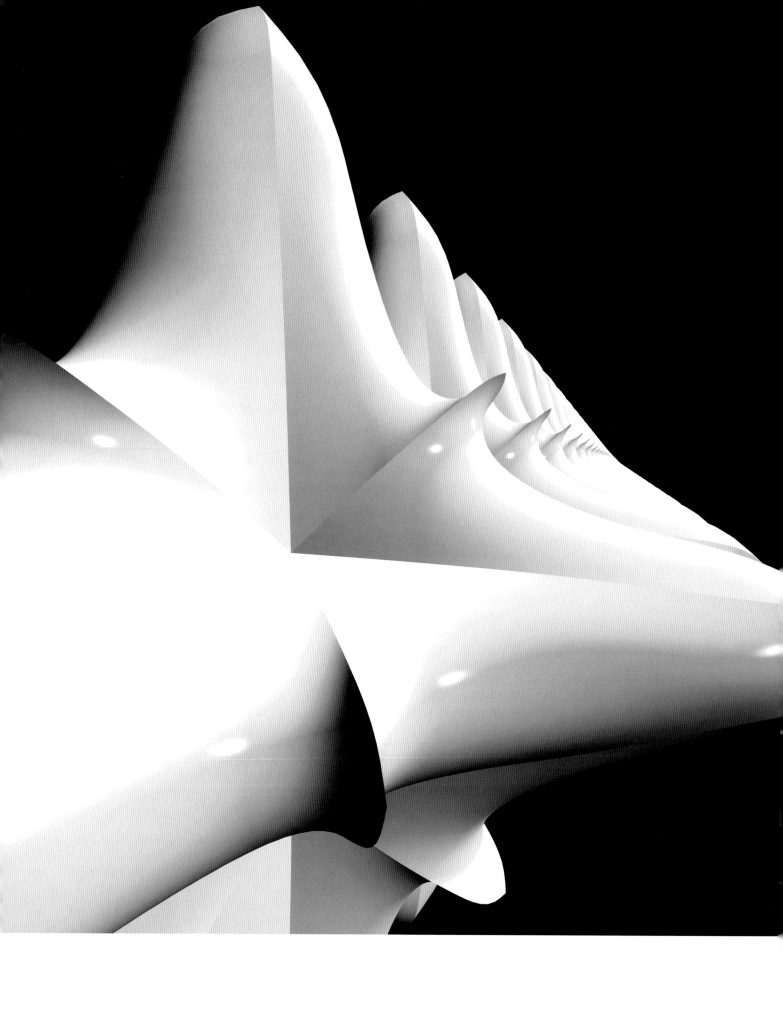

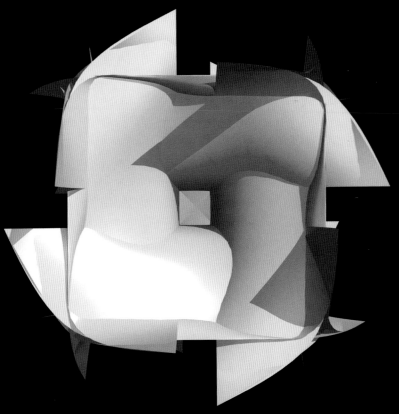

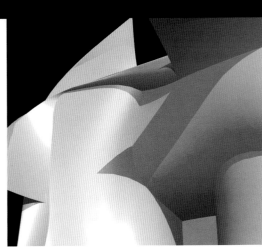

that they share common denominators for the description of their component surfaces. Through the use of low-level computer programming the component surfaces are altered in space so that their topological arrangement is not altered whereas the forms they describe are. The cube-to-sphere surface on the bottom left of page 8 shows the arrangement for morphing a cube into a sphere: the four triangular faces that are the subcomponents of each of the six faces to the cube become rounded, each tending towards the 24 curved components that make up the sphere. The cube-to-cylinder surface on the bottom right of page 8 shows the same schema for morphing a cube into a sphere.

This is an architectural problem, not one of computer science. From an educational point of view inhabitants (participants) are forced into examining the geometry for each of the forms in absolute terms, and also in relative terms in order to construct the transformation of one to another.

Worlds are about community and in Our World we seek to manage hybridisation collectively. Commonality therefore has required that the structure of representation, and accordingly change, is based on a democratically equal starting point: 24 component surfaces contiguously combining together to form a closed volume. Each vertex can be given a name, as can the edges between adjacent surfaces even when the edges disappear by definition, as is the case of the sphere. We have compromised artificially in order to speak the same language by not speaking different languages that otherwise might have emerged in this collective creative enterprise.

Such simplicity soon becomes problematic. If we morph the cube that has six faces to a pyramid with five, for instance, the difficulty we have created is obvious: how do we cope programmatically with the reduction and eventual disappearance of one of the faces – the top face of the cube which tends towards the pyramidal point? At what 'point' (in time and in space) does the face disappear, and what is the nature of its disappearance?

Using low-level programming skills – as much as an architect might desire to possess – this conundrum cannot be dealt with cleanly: the offending face needs to appear to disappear yet still exist, much in the way that the elaborate chests within chests in *The Third Policeman* reduce in scale, becoming invisible to the eye of the observer but not with respect to the craft of the policeman who has charged himself with miniaturising artifice in ever-decreasing scale.[4]

The reason for the retention of the face is the open-ended nature of the formal conversation. Hybrid series one (cube -→ sphere) might be followed sequentially (as opposed to separately) by hybrid series two (sphere -→ pyramid). For series two to pick up from the consequences of the preceding series one, the

to lay out the iterative changes (morphs) in an organised environment. As a collection we have mapped an environment defined by its contents. The general layout on the top of page 8 shows the context – Our World. The name is a means to ensure that the hybrid design environment has an identity, and the particularity of its choice is just that: a domain ('World') whose collaborative ('Our') artificial construction is no more than a means to represent physically relationships between objects generated through an iterative process of change.

Having constructed a world we need to construct spatial linkages with attendant hierarchies; a system based on a Cartesian grid serves us well. Consequently the three axes have a Phileban form at each end, a total of six with an additional seventh form being the cube in the centre that acts as the initiator. The central cube simply matches the inevitable Cartesian limits for the world created.

The first step is to define a set of characteristics for each of the seven forms so hybridising operation needs to continue using identifiable commonalities: 24 faces and their geometrical description. If we simply 'disappear' a redundant face, its subsequent reappearance cannot be guaranteed.

If Our World were Flatland, filling it with objects relies on a pattern of two sequential operations. This is shown arbitrarily in figure 2. The X-axis shows an example of one particular route. The initial cube is tending towards a sphere along the positive X-axis. At an intermediate point the resultant 'sphericised cubical' form then tends towards a wedge along the positive Y-axis. Taking Our World from Flatland to three dimensions, the 'wedgical spherical cube' can be further hybridised, in this case towards a pyramid along the positive Z-axis.

If we confined ourselves to Flatland (XY plane), we could generate a set of hybrids where, to any given number, the plane could be populated by a set of cube to sphere/wedge/cylinder/cone hybrids. Each unique object would be generated in a unique sequence, conforming to an X -→ Y-→ Z order of hybridisation. In a set involving 15 hybrid steps 3/15 -→ sphere, say, followed by 7/15 -→ wedge followed by 11/15 -→ pyramid produces a slightly different hybrid than 3/15 -→ sphere followed by 8/15 -→ wedge followed by 11/15 -→ pyramid. The number of iterations determines the population. In the case given above, the population would be 15 number X+ combining with 14 X-, which totals 29 for the X-axis. This could be matched by 29 for the Y-axis. The population of Flatland in this case would be 29^2, which totals 841 unique objects.

Moving to the three-dimensional world we can fill the volume by augmenting the sequence used to populate Flatland, but adding a third operation along the Z-axis. The population for Our World would be 29^3 in this example, which totals 24,389 unique objects.

Animating the sequence at 15 iterations per second could generate an illusion of seamless transition to the eye. In this way the cube–sphere morph composed of 15 iterative hybrid steps would take one second to reveal.

Taxonomists will recognise that Our World is little more than a collector's regime where sets of objects can be filed in rows of vertical shelving to facilitate cataloguing for subsequent investigations into similarity and difference. This Cartesian spatial management of varieties is little more, then, than a library or a museologist's specimen store. We are trapped by the artificial limits of working with pure forms only, as indeed we are by constraining ourselves

to the limit of three sequences that are metaphorically and practically tied to a spatial arrangement based on three dimensions. If we go beyond the whole, in other words make a 16th hybrid object from the cube -→ sphere morph based on 15 iterations, we produce an object that is first in a line that goes beyond the purely spherical towards a swollen sphere and, worse from the cataloguer's point of view, one that is outside the domain of Our World. It is in some outer space which, compared to Our World, has no limits.

Computational collapse is easy to induce by seeking the generation of objects deep beyond the Phileban-form pattern. Equally, if we four-dimensionalise the generation of population by introducing a fourth hybrid operational series, or five-six-n-dimensionalise the generation, where can we store the objects? Here our tidy universe collapses …

'Did you ever happen to visit the cinematograph in your travels?'
'Never,' I answered humbly, 'but I believe it is a dark quarter and little can be seen at all except the photographs on the wall.'[5]

In teaching architecture one often ponders on what today's student, released by the computer from the hours of hatching and other manual craft-based time-consumers prevalent in traditional architectural study, does in their stead. What should we offer in their place, of equivalent usefulness and less excruciating time commitment?

Computer programming is one possibility, and I argue that it provides an opportunity for students to understand the potential of the instrument in a more knowledgeable light. Using software packages originally intended for the film industry uncritically, they otherwise too easily rely on the artfulness of the software writers and their packages of pre-formed algorithms for geometrical game-playing and illusions of movement. Our World is necessarily work in progress with wider implications still to be tracked. At a specific level it looks at cooperative enterprise that seeks a broader understanding of the 'great plan', indeed the world in which we find ourselves, in the context of a vague awareness of, and even familiarity with, our pre-existence or fears of postmortal irrelevance. Animation as a technique of illusion is relatively hopeless in helping to advance spatial understanding within the confines of three dimensions, still less the spatial implications of multidimensional mathematics that go beyond the third. Just as the Third Policeman remains elusive throughout the novel of his namesake, architecturally the allegorical potential and practical implications of animation remain elusive, however much we disguise time as the constituent fourth dimension. ⌀

Notes
1. Flann O'Brien, *The Third Policeman*, Picador (London), edition, 1974.
2. Ibid, p 173.
3. Although the publishers do their best to do so themselves by providing, at the conclusion of the novel, a revealing quote from a letter to William Saroyan written by the author on completion of his work.
4. Op cit, pp 61–64.
5. Ibid, p 52.

Credits and acknowledgements:
Explanatory models and rendering: the author and Simon Anson. 'Our World' renditions and probes: modelled by the author, rendered by Grant Dunlop. Research and layout: Grant Dunlop. The author notes his appreciation for the SRC421 class (1998) who so wholeheartedly formed the Our World community.

'A record of this belief will be found in the literature of all ancient peoples. There are four winds and eight sub-winds, each with its own colour. The wind from the east is a deep purple, from the south a fine shining silver. The north wind is a hard black and west is amber. People in the old days had the power of perceiving these colours and could spend a day sitting quietly on a hillside watching the beauty of the winds, their fall and rise and changing hues, the magic of neighbouring winds when they are inter-weaved like ribbons at a wedding. It was a better occupation than gazing at newspapers. The sub-winds had colours of indescribable delicacy, reddish-yellow halfway between silver and purple, a greyish-green which was related equally to black and brown. What could be more exquisite than a countryside swept lightly by cool rain reddened by the south-west breeze!'
Flann O'Brien, *The Third Policeman*, pp 28–29.

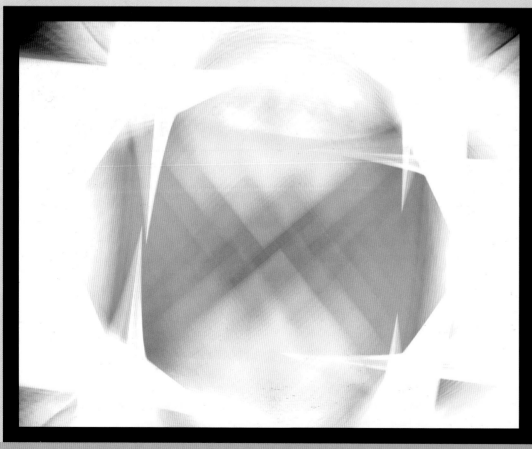

'He made it himself secretly in the backyard, very likely in the cowhouse. It was very thin and slight like the very finest of spider's muslin. You would not see it at all if you held it against the sky but at certain angles of the light you might at times accidentally notice the edge of it. It was the purest and most perfect manifestation of the outside skin of light yellow. This yellow was the colour of my birth-wind.' Flann O'Brien, *The Third Policeman*, p 29.

'Every time my birthday came,' old Mathers said, 'I was presented with another little gown of the same identical quality except that it was put on over the other one and not in place of it. You may appreciate the extreme delicacy and fineness of the material when I tell you that even at five years old with five of these gowns together on me, I still appeared to be naked. It was, however, an unusual yellowish sort of nakedness. Of course there was no objection to wearing other clothes over the gown. I usually wore an overcoat. But every year I got a new gown.' Flann O Brien, *The Third Policeman*, p 30.

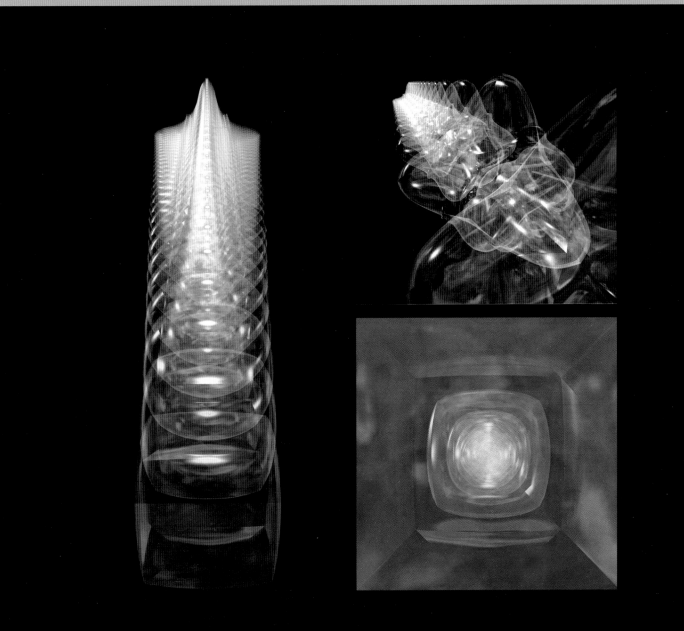

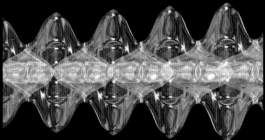

'Yes. Since you will be wearing as a grown man the tiny gown that fitted you when you were born, it is clear that the gown has stretched until it is perhaps one hundred times as big as it was originally. Naturally this will affect the colour, making it many times rarer than it was. Similarly there will be a proportionate stretch and a corresponding diminution in colour in all the gowns up to manhood – perhaps twenty or so in all.'
Flann O Brien, *The Third Policeman*, pp 30–31.

'There is also Sergeant Pluck and another man called
MacCruiskeen and there is a third man called Fox that
disappeared twenty-five years ago and was never heard
of after. The first two are down in the barracks and so far
as I know they have been there for hundreds of years. They
must be operating on a very rare colour, something that
ordinary eyes could not see at all. There is no white wind
that I know of. They all have the gift of seeing the winds.'
(Flann O'Brien, *The Third Policeman*, p 31)

Anodyne

In architecture, animation techniques are generally confined to the generative design process. Few occasions arise in which architects are able to focus their creative talents on their own built work. However, Anodyne, a collaboration with DJ Spooky, presented Bernard Tschumi with the unique opportunity of making his own Lerner Hall — completed in 1999 by Bernard Tschumi Architects for Columbia University — the subject of a multimedia exhibition. Ali Rahim posed a series of questions to Tschumi, centred around Lerner Hall and his approach to animation.

Bernard Tschumi and Paul Miller (aka DJ Spooky) worked together on a piece exhibited at the Venice Biennale 2000. It was an unusual collaboration between an architect and a musical and visual artist. Bernard Tschumi had been asked to exhibit images of movement in space in one of his new buildings, Lerner Hall. Yet he felt that showing photographs or models would not convey the idea of action and interaction that the inside of the building was about. DJ Spooky, an artist, writer and musician working in New York, worked with images and film footage from Lerner Hall and expanded from

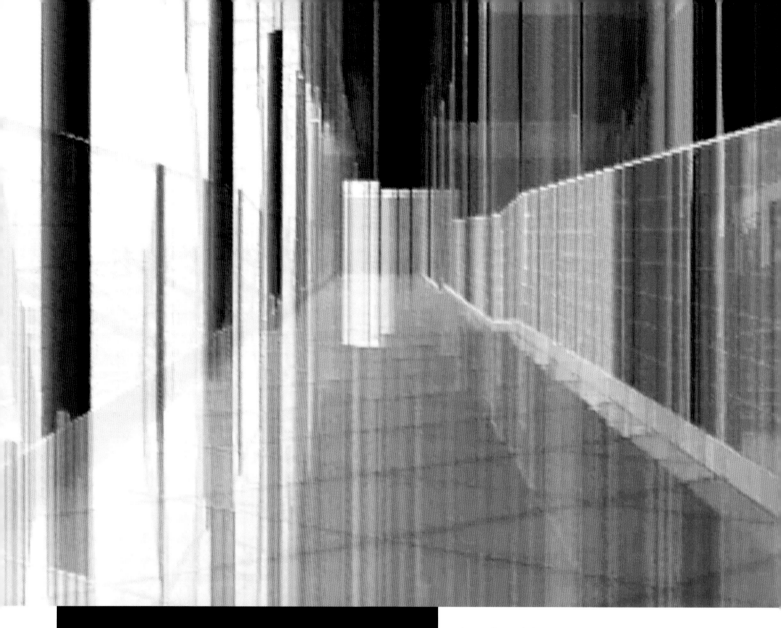

them. One of the most striking moments was when he derived music electronically, based on a set of drawings of the glass ramps. The result takes the building one step further, into the realm of music and media culture.

Lerner Hall, designed as the new student centre for Columbia University in New York, is about mixing the old and the new, mixing spaces and event. It combines a historical context: the 1880s Neoclassical master plan of McKim, Mead and White with its bricks and stone, and an unusual set of suspended glass ramps linking the more conventional parts of the building. The ramps are a place of encounter and social interaction. They lead you to a 1,100-seat auditorium, a cinema, an experimental theatre, rehearsal rooms, food places and so on. New technologies were used to build the ramps so that they hold a large glass wall and people are constantly onstage as they walk up and down them.

Conversation: Ali Rahim with Bernard Tschumi

Ali Rahim:The notation systems or duration within cinematic processes is the moment of maximum creativity within cinematic sequence. This process of difference is not reliant on the form of the diagram or its quantity, but the qualitative influences that the diagram produces. Is the use of cinema analogy in your work similar to John Cage's notation systems where these diagrams can be interpreted but contain an element of chance?

Bernard Tschumi: In architecture, movement notation can document both vectorised movement (for example, ramps, corridors) and random movement (evident in open spaces). The element of chance is inherent to nonvectorised movement. The same differentiation can apply to the use of the building, its program and activities.

AR: Does chance influence your design method – or is it a controlled contamination or emergence of terms and ideas such as 'transprogramming', 'disprogramming' and 'crossprogramming'? If it is a controlled

narrative as well as creation, similar to Dziga Vertov's ideas of cinematic sequence, or do you use media to explore the possibilities of nonhierarchical organisations that influence your concepts?

BT: Both.

AR: Moving from potential creativity to an actualised manifestation of a project, the coding of all nonhierarchical heterogeneities are controlled by designing conditions that result in particular spatial configurations and form. Do you see these as choreographies of unfolding sequences of cinematic experience or dynamic stabilities as opposed to static built forms?

BT: I define architecture as the encounter of space, event and movement. Hence, it is inevitably about

emergence, then are the effects of their manifestation greater than initially predicted?

BT: Our intention is not to condition design (even with chance strategies) but rather to design conditions so as to allow for chance encounters or programmatic collisions. Their manifestations are always more or less than initially predicted, as architecture is inevitably subverted by some of its uses or users.

AR: These contaminations and their effects are reliant on nonhierarchical ideas such as actions, spaces and movements. What are the implications of designing for a changing use and temporality of these events? Are you suggesting that we move well beyond typology towards a condition that invents and reinvents simultaneously, where architecture becomes an active participant?

BT: Typology presupposes canonic forms. Topology would be a better term, insofar as the fluidity and adjacency of spaces can affect the nature of events.

AR: What part do different modes of representation such as animations play in the investigation or manifestation of such ideas? Do you see simulations as being informative of

dynamic sequences of movement unfolding within static sequences of spaces.

AR: Are these heterogeneous flows and oscillations manifested at all scales simultaneously? For example, Lerner Hall is both a stage for the play of the activities of the inside seen from below, but also acts as a proscenium to the theatre of the city beyond its walls. The ramps that hold the theatre's stage and its viewers also hold the glass curtain that falls between the campus and the building. How does this mediation simultaneously reflect in construction techniques and the materiality of the building?

BT: Lerner Hall's construction technology is as normative as the technology of its 'contextual' facades, with the intended exception of the suspended glass ramps. I often like to say that the place of the concept should also be the place of technological invention.

AR: Are Lerner Hall's effects greater than expected? The cycles of programmed activities operate like John Cage's notation system. Now duration has moved to being one of collapsing the past, present and future – reinventing our experience. DJ Spooky has performed this system of simultaneity, but how do we as architects move beyond this reinvention?

BT: The next building we design is always meant to be the most inventive one. ⌂

Credits:
Conversation with
Bernard Tschumi,
Research Assistant:
John How

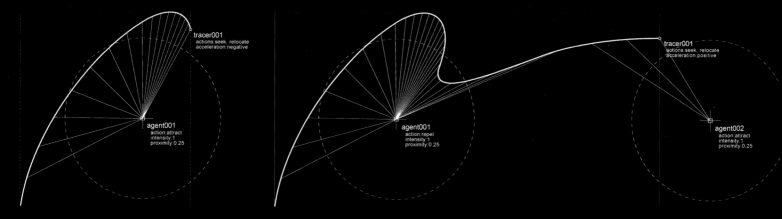

tracer001
actions:seek, relocate
acceleration:negative

agent001
action:attract
intensity:1
proximity:0.25

tracer001
actions:seek, relocate
acceleration:positive

agent001
action:repel
intensity:1
proximity:0.25

agent002
action:attract
intensity:1
proximity:0.25

Animated Techniques:
Time and the Technological
Acquiescence of Animation

With the recent adoption of animation techniques, time has become an inherent preoccupation in architecture. Through the work of early 20th-century experimental animators Hans Richter, Alexander Alexeieff and Norman McLaren, Gregory More traces the treatment of time through animation technologies. He then puts forward an alternative reading of time associated with the architectural use of parametric design.

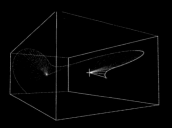

Above and right
Agents and tracers: Every agent is given a particular set of locally specific actions triggered by the proximity of a tracer. Behaviours are structured as components of information, conditional to the local or global, cumulative and transmittable, interagent or intertracer. The tracers are also infused with their own sets of characteristics, or reactions, establishing a dialogue between tracer and agent, where effect becomes causative.

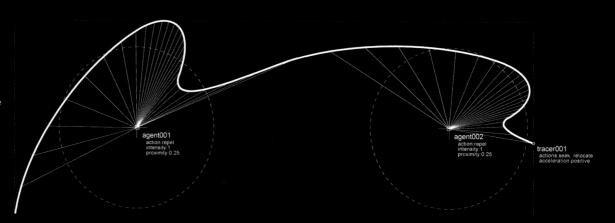

agent001
action:repel
intensity:1
proximity:0.25

agent002
action:repel
intensity:1
proximity:0.25

tracer001
actions:seek, relocate
acceleration:positive

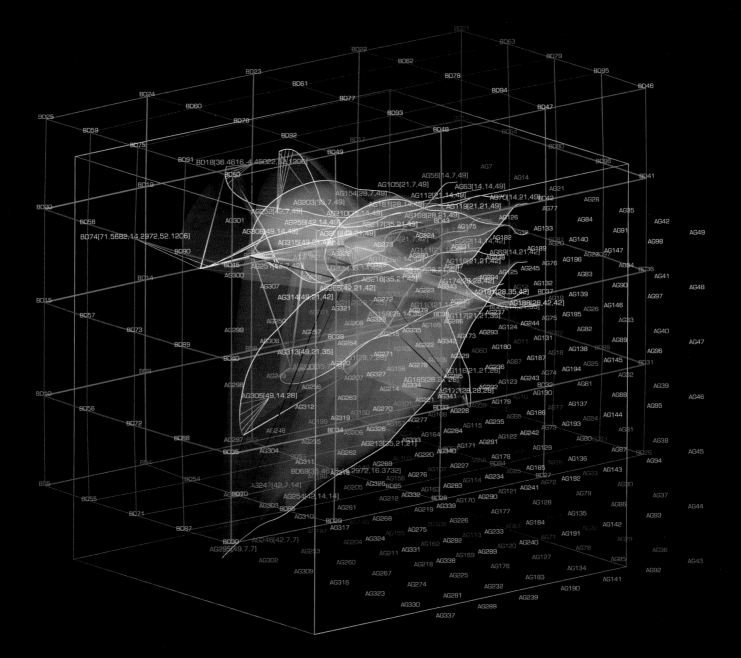

Above
A causative environment is established that incorporates both corporeal (form based) and incorporeal (informational) modes of operation. Agents are released into varied and varying configurations which serve as reactive spatial geographies. The tracers are released into these reactive matrices.

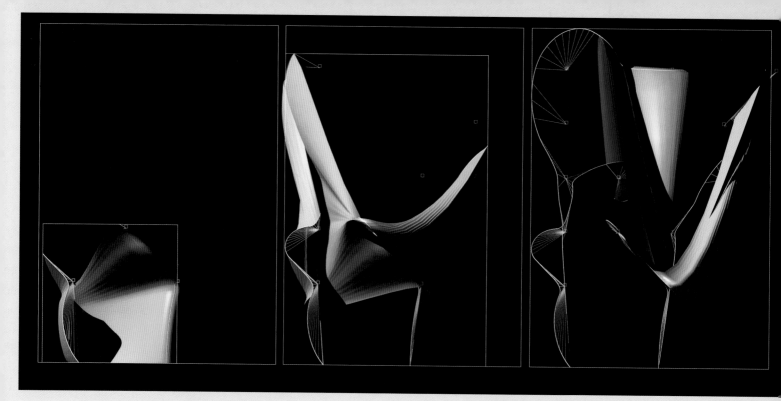

Animation as a visual prosthetic encourages generative and perceptive transformations to a body of architectural work. Located tacitly within a scopic regime of form-making this body exhibits an openness to technological change. An attendant predilection to animate architectural form is nourished by the utilisation of animation technologies. As a consequence the discipline of architecture has been reconditioned, be it quantitatively or qualitatively, with the inclusion of 'time' as an inherent dimension. It is this acceptance of time and its technological implications within architectural form-making that require further examination.

The art-form of animation emerged from a crisis in the visual arts at the beginning of the twentieth century. The crisis occurred when visual artists, predominately painters, explored creative form relative to time. Their explorations were encouraged by an understanding and application of contemporary developments in cinematic techniques. The significant difference between the canvas based art and the technical requirements of animated imagery caused a divergence that in turn created the art-form known as animation. The following investigation into experimental animation begins from this artistic divergence, or alternatively, from the technological acquiescence of animation.

So what relevance does an architectural reading into the development of experimental animation have, when both visual aesthetics and technologies have advanced well beyond these primary efforts? Tracing the introduction of time into an art-form reveals a commonality in artistic and technological causality. The art-form of animation has furthered the perceptual qualities of time beyond the ability of the static arts. Similarly animation and animation software have allowed architects to embellish architectural form beyond the techniques of inert media. The production of time-based architectural form, with animation techniques, however, incorporates the cinematic mechanisms of relating imagery to quantified and unitised notions of time. This promotes a question: which technologies within the realm of architecture today, other than animation software, provide opportunities to create difference in the conception of time based form and its relationship to architectural production? The architectural use of parametric design and associative-geometry modelling tools are examined here to present an alternative reading of time in architectural representation, form, and technology: a contrast to cinematic modulation, which seems to be the backbone of contemporary time based architectural design.

Visual Plasticity

The ability of animation to metamorphose freely in both form and narrative lends itself to being one of the most imaginative methods of artistic expression.[1] Coupling this freedom of expression with associated technical requirements has made animation difficult to classify and define in its relationship to traditional art genres.[2] A recent architectural comparison to the art of animation focused on the art of character animation and the properties of mutability.[3] This examination of character follows a trait that animation is generally associated with anthropomorphism, an association due significantly to the popularity of studios such as Disney that mainstreamed the art form into popular culture.[4] Quite separate to the emergence of the cartoon industry were the reticent kinetic art explorations begun in the

Above and opposite
The accommodation of memory or *memoria technica* allows for the visualisation of change over time. Surfaces, lines and points demarcate the interaction between agents and tracers. The result forms a hyperhistorical surfacing of informational interaction.

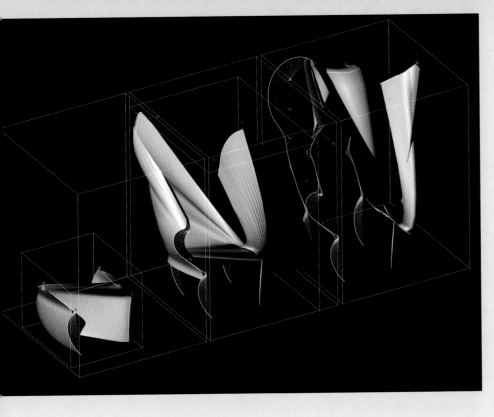

Aionic Memoria
The Stoic notions of Chronos and Aion are the premise for this architectonic proposition. As two contrasting readings of time, Chronos and Aion provide a dualistic metaphor for the enduring and the provisional, the anticipated and the unexpected, the bodily and the incorporeal. If considered reductively, these Stoic readings of time present the difference between continuous (Chronos) and discrete change (Aion). Aionic Memoria seeks to encourage and trace a dialogue between Chronos and Aion through an architectural amalgamation of animation and programming. Causative environments are established and tracers are released into these matrices of change. Sense of vision becomes fallible in an environment of discrete vacillating computational singularities. The visual continuum of animation is agitated beyond its perceptual limits. This sensorial fallibility, a state of optical nervousness, is the result of creating a spatial matrix based on volatile and provisional events. An informational *memoria technica* enables the tracing of movement and change within this causative space, sedating an otherwise infinitely nonregulated condition. The surfaces, lines and points are the *visulisation* of this informational memory; they bring forth the past, present and, ultimately, future. A complex, if not perplex, reading of time through form and space. This hyper(historical) surfacing reveals the continuity of change over time, realising its corporeality from the tracery of incorporeal events.

second decade of the 20th century which were defined as 'experimental animations'.[5] The use of the term 'experimental' denotes the innovative and explorative techniques used to create new types and methods of animation.

The first known artistic creation of an abstract animation was by the painter Leopold Survage in 1912. Survage was inspired to create his work of animation, entitled 'Rhythm-colour symphonies in movement', by contemporary trends in abstract and Cubist painting. Guillaume Apollinaire, art critic and poet, wrote that Survage had 'invented a new art of painting in motion', which was about to manifest itself by means of cinema. Apollinaire was convinced by the determining influence of science and mathematics in shaping the new departure proposed by Cubist painting:

Today scientists no longer limit themselves to the three dimensions of the Euclid. The painters have been quite naturally, one might say by intuition, to preoccupy themselves with new possibilities of spatial measurement which, in the language of modern studios, are designated by the term: the fourth dimension. Regarded from the plastic point of view, the fourth dimension appears to spring from the other three known dimensions; it represents the immensity of space eternalising itself, the dimensions of the infinite; the fourth dimension endows objects with plasticity.[6]

The 'fourth dimension' became an ambiguous definition, a catch phrase of sorts, that embraced dimensionality from simply the combination of space and time to that of Einstein's curved space. Recent architectural discussions have shared a similar fascination with concepts of multidimensionality.[7] It was the perception of an added temporal dimension within art that endowed objects and forms with the sense of plasticity. A 'new plasticity'[8] emerged in the early decades of the 20th century as an all encompassing condition rather than a material definition. It is within this period that Apollinaire was writing about the plasticity of form encouraged by the rethinking of aesthetics, sciences, and technology in regard to new conceptions of space and time. Survage's theorisation of an abstract animation also occurred within this milieu, where time and technology were seen as integral to the advancement of concepts in the arts.

Between 1912 and 1914 Survage painted more than 200 watercolour plates and sketches for his animation. The contents of the coloured plates were abstract in nature with compositions consisting of curved forms that appeared free and weightless without a sense of gravity or materiality. Although Survage published his ideas, registered his animation work at the Academy of Sciences in Paris and teamed up with a company who were pioneering a colour-film processing technique, his artwork was never animated. His 'Rhythm-colour symphonies in movement' were never cinematically photographed and aligned to a mechanism of systemised time, never endowed with the plasticity they were produced to reveal.[9]

Time and Composition
In the 1920s the artists Walter Ruttman, Hans Richter and Viking Eggeling made key developments in the kinetic art-form frequently categorised as 'experimental film'.[10] Richter and Eggeling's static serial paintings on canvas were an obvious precursor to their later animation projects. Linear painted sequences of

Notes
1. 'Some would argue that it [metamorphosis] is the constituent core of animation itself.' Paul Wells, *Understanding Animation*, Routledge (London), 1998, p 69.
2. For a scope of the wide-ranging definitions of animation refer to Jane Pilling (ed), *A Reader in Animation Studies*, John Libbey (Sydney), 1997; produced by The Society of Animation Studies (SAS).
3. Mark Rakatansky, 'Motivations of animation', *Architecture New York*, no 23 (1998), p 50.
4. John Berger, 'Francis Bacon and Walt Disney' in *Ways of Seeing*, Writers and Readers (London), 1972; and Simon Pummell, 'Francis Bacon and Walt Disney revisited', in Pilling, *A Reader in Animation Studies*. John Berger makes insightful comparisons between the work of Walt Disney and the work of painter Francis Bacon in a provocative linking between 'low art' and 'high art' which breaks down certain cultural assumptions about both artists. Simon Pummell takes this discussion into the realm of animation theory by referencing Bacon's use of Muybridge's motion photographs and Disney's techniques of animation.
5. Robert Russett, *Experimental Animation*, Van Nostrand Reinhold (New York), 1976.
6. CH Waddington, *Behind*

abstracted and diagrammatic compositions were positioned on single elongated canvases termed 'scrolls'. Tschumi utilised a similar diagrammatic and sequenced drawing technique to convey architectural transformation in his Manhattan Transcripts project. This sequenced or cinematic approach presents an evolving plasticity between event and environment, a fluidity that relies on the human eye to mediate the transformation and transition between static images. Richter and Eggeling's scrolls also relied on human mediation. The scrolls present their first steps towards an abstracted mutable aesthetic which they were to develop further in their experimental animations:

> It was not only the orchestration of form but also of time-relationship that we were facing in film. The single image disappeared in a flow of images, which made sense only if it helped to articulate a new element – time.[11]

The transition between the static cinematic qualities of the painted scrolls and the actuality of an animated film required the incorporation of a new dimension: time. This incorporation also required the application of cinematic techniques in the production of a multitude of varying graphical compositions and their serial photography. The animate image becomes 'enframed' by burdens of imaging multiplicity and accommodating the cinematic apparatus. Both Richter and Eggeling relied on musical metaphors to interpret this new temporal medium: rhythm, harmony, instrument and orchestration were terms used to describe properties of animated film.[12] Composition was now a term used not only in its graphical sense but also in its temporal musical sense. Time, through the hybrid medium of the 'film-canvas', tended to be treated with metronomic precision, calculating change and action to specific quantities of frames.[13] The generation of the imagery for Richter and Eggeling's animations remained pedagogically based in the art of painting. It was in the following decades that experimental animators developed image generating techniques that diverged from traditional methods found in the painted arts.

Movement Tracery
'An illusory solid is the course run during a given length of time by a real solid, called a generator or tracer.' Alexander Alexeieff in the 1950s developed an animation method based on illusory solids that relied on long photographic

exposures. He designed an apparatus to relate the movement of rotating tracers to the exposure of the camera. Etienne Marey had undertaken similar studies in the 1880s with revolving solids and multiple-exposure photographs.[14] Alexeieff, however, used these photographic images to create frames of animation. Each frame of the animation captured the complete movement of the tracer, with the visualised form varying with each adjustment of the tracer's path. This is an interesting corollary to Marey's or Eadweard Muybridge's decomposition of movement through instantaneous photography. The latter revealed the difference between the instants of time, whereas Alexeieff's technique revealed the difference between durations of traced movement.

Norman McLaren's 1969 Pas de Deux expresses the latent qualities of ballet by visualising a multiplicity of movement.[15] White-clad dancers were filmed in front of a black backdrop with their figures delineated by backlighting so their bodies appear as white silhouettes. McLaren made multiple re-exposures of the film, with each re-exposure being stepped or offset to the previous one, so the actions of the dancers are overlaid and appear slightly out of synchronisation. When action occurs an average of eleven images are revealed, all at different stages of movement. The silhouetted ballerinas fan and decay into and out of volumes of movement, vividly tracing the trajectory of each limb with their unique delays and pauses. Each movement folds into the next, with sublime richness and variety. This ghosting of animate form visualises the dancer's ability to demarcate space and volume, giving the illusion that their movement is occurring through a charged and phosphorescent space.

Both Alexieff and Mclaren's animations deal with the visual interpretation of existing or traced movement. They capture moving three-dimensional figures in space and, by tracing or overlaying action, give vision to a previously nonexistent form. This visualisation is reliant on the precise relationship between time and image: be it by postproduction frame-based techniques or by developing machines that relate camera action to movement. These examples display animation's technological dependence on the quantified reduction of time to a unitised dimension. With the mechanism of cinema reconstituting movement by aligning images to time, or as Henri Bergson stated 'immobile section + abstracted time'.[16] The animate and inanimate become divided by the presence or absence of the cinematic apparatus.

Varying Time
The pioneering and experimental animation techniques of the last century may seem somewhat arduous when compared to methods that can be simulated with contemporary animation software. The visualisation

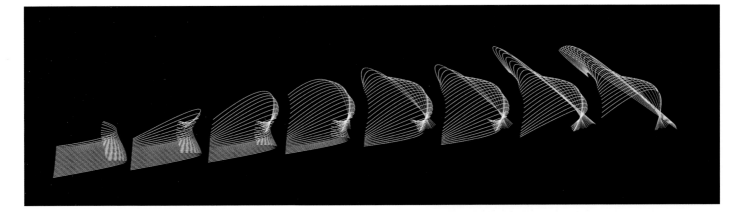

Appearance, MIT Press (Cambridge, Mass, 1969), p 15. Guillaume Apollinaire is quoted by Waddington in this study of the relationships between painting and the natural sciences in the 20th century.

7. These multidimensional concepts have sponsored a counterargument where Euclidean geometry is examined to reveal challenging spatial configurations without the need to delve into multidimensionality. See Bernard Cache, 'A plea for Euclid', *ANY*, no 24 (1998).

8. Sanford Kwinter, *La Citta Nuova: Modernity and Continuity*, Zone 1–2, Urzone (New York), 1986.

9. 59 of the plates are owned by MOMA in New York, 12 are in the *Cinémathéque Francaise*, and the others are owned by family and artist-friends. Russett, op cit, p 43.

10. 'This form, of all cinematic institutions, is the one which is consciously most akin to the "plastic arts" (to the point that today experimental films are exhibited in museums of modern art).' Jacques Aumont, *The Image*, British Film Institute (London) 1997, p 208.

11. Hans Richter, *Magazine of Art* (February 1952), in R Russett, op cit, p 110.

12. For the computational and the musical see Marcos Novak, 'Transmittable Architecture', in Martin Pearce and Neil Spiller *Architects in Cyberspace*, Architectural Design, vol 65, no 12, 1995.

13. 'In any case we should remember that while the eye, particularly the well-trained eye of the film-maker or the critic, can discern plastic composition in space, it is by nature much less able to perceive the flow of time. This has been noted by many film theorists from Eisenstein (who derides "metrical montage" as early as 1929) to Jean Mitry, who devotes a chapter to the question in Esthetique et psychologie du cinema (1963–65).' Aumont, op cit, p 208.

14. Laurent Mannoni, Etienne-Jules Marey, *Cinémathéque Francaise* (Paris) 1999, p 220. It is no coincidence that the photographic images of Marey's rotating tracers create images of second-order

tools of animation software include a range from traditional cinematic techniques to those of a scientific or mathematical paradigm. The latter utilises the continued advancements in the mathematical understanding and calculation of form. Fluid modellers and force-driven deformation algorithms are a selection of these animation features, used by architects to explore the generation of animate form. These techniques are located within a scientific paradigm of change, where time is quantifiable and reducible.[17] However, alternative technologies accessible to architects exist which illuminate a differing relationship between time, technology and architectural representation. Parametric design with associative geometry software[18] or, less easy to define, the unique use of programming or coding of form are such technologies that diverge from the dominance of cinematic visualisation.

Bernard Cache and his Paris-based company Objectile utilise parametric design within modes of architectural production. Alignments with fabrication technologies allow Objectile to create highly variable component-based architectural objects: acoustic panels, table surfaces and glass screens. The ability to manipulate form rapidly through parametrically variable software allows a variety of complex physical objects to be fabricated directly from a highly flexible digital model. For one of Objectile's Web-based projects animation becomes a visualisation tool, for user selection, illuminating the variety of alternatives. Although the animation is purely cinematic, it visualises a transformation of form directly tied to processes of fabrication and economics of production. Animation is a by-product of working with systems of variability and adaptability. Time becomes a complex element when designing within nonstandard modes of production tied to material and fabrication constraints.

Cache's 'objectile' is a contemporary conception of a technological object. Where the idea of the 'standard' object is replaced by an object that assumes a place in a continuum through variation, and where industrial automation or serial machinery replaces stamped form.[19] The technological replacement

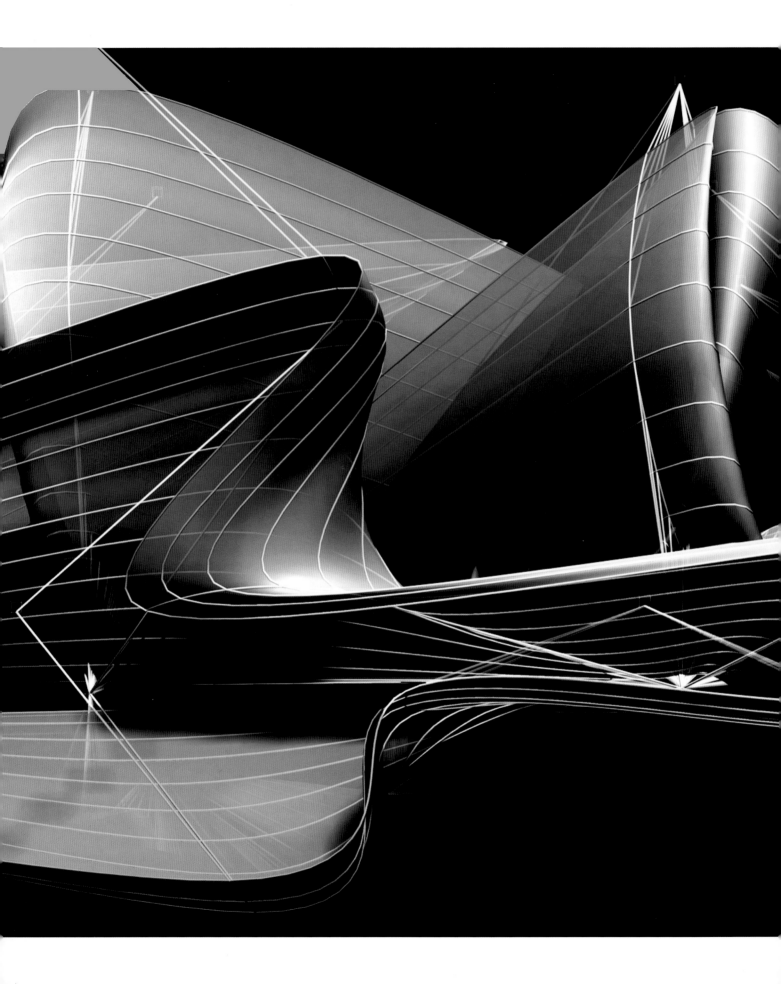

geometry (specifically hyperboloids) which can be described by straight lines, as the rotating illusory solids relied on straight-line tension.
15. The Ether/I project by Paris-based dECOi architects captured the movements of dancers as the generative force for an architectonic sculpture for UNESCO's 50th anniversary.
16. H Bergson, *Creative Evolution*, Macmillan (London), 1911, p 361.
17. David Rodowick, *Gilles Deleuze's Time Machine*, Duke University Press (Durham, NC), 1997, p 21. Rodowick presents the reducible and the irreducible as 'the difference between calculating the formula for the trajectory of falling bodies and the unique event of a meteor exhausting itself in the earth's atmosphere'.
18. For exploration of the potentials of parametric design refer to Mark Burry, 'Paramorph: anti-accident methodologies' in Stephen Perella (ed), Hypersurface Architecture II, *Architectural Design*, vol 69, no 9–10, 1999.
19. Gilles Deleuze, *The Fold: Leibniz and the Baroque*, The Athlone Press (London), 1993, p 19.
20. Bernard Cache, *Earth Moves*, MIT Press (Cambridge, Mass), 1995, pp 39–41.

that transforms the conception of the architectural 'object' is comparable to the cinematic apparatus giving rise to animation: an art-form whose actualisation transpired through an openness to technological change. With the architectural engagement of animation software we have witnessed the development of concepts incorporating time that are inherently tied to the cinematic model of thought. This has encouraged the visual predicament between the digitally animated and the physically inanimate. Change in architectural form becomes defined relative to frames of animation and time is treated as an applied dimension that is readily removed for the procurement of physical form: the freeze frame. The technologies of parametric design diverge from this cinematic treatment of time, and they in turn require a reconsideration of what this divergence means within the discipline of architecture. Working from a suggestion by Cache, time within these technologies could be thought as varying, as opposed to flowing, like the surface of the geographer – 'that science of the nudity of surfaces', with the varying depths of investigation.[20] This is an alternative conceptual reading of time, which disturbs the flow of cinematic modulation. ⌂

Irreducible Time:

Main picture
Perspective of project in site.

Inset
Formal strategies informed
by animation technique.

As guest editor of the *Contemporary Processes in Architecture* title of *Architectural Design* (vol 70, no 3, 2000), Ali Rahim expounded the importance of maximising on the creative potential of 'systemic delay' in the digitalised design process. Here he describes how certain animation techniques can optimise on the unpredictable, irreversible and qualitative manner of time.

Machining Possibilities

THE MALL

CAPITALISM IS DEPENDENT ON GOVERNMENT POLICIES, AND IS HIERARCHICAL. THE MESHWORK OF
CAPITALISM AND ITS INFLUENCES IS AT THE CROSSROADS OF ALL TYPES OF FORMATIONS . THESE
INFLUENCES ATTRIBUTED TO LOCAL CONDITIONS DEVELOP SPONTANEOUSLY AT VARIEGATED MOMENTS.
THIS CONCEPTUAL UNDERPINNING OF THE PROJECT INFORMED THE TECHNIQUE OF THE ANIMATION.

ABSTRACT MACHINE

THE HIERARCHIES OF IK CHAINS ARE RELIANT ON THE PROCESS OF FLOWS AS MOBILIZED FORCE,
WHICH REFERS TO THE DETERRITORIALIZATION OF THE MARKETPLACE. PRECISE COMBINATIONS
INHERENT IN THE SHAPING AND TUNING OF THIS TECHNIQUE ARTICULATED QUANTITATIVE AND
QUALITATIVE INFLUENCES THAT MAXIMIZED POTENTIAL.

TECHNIQUE

THE TECHNIQUE PROVIDED US WITH A MATRIX OF NEW IDEAS OF MAKING AT ALL SCALES. AS THE
FORM AND ORGANIZATION OF THE IK CHAINS MOVED TO A FIELD OF POTENTIAL THAT WAS RELATIONAL
AND SCALELESS. OUR INITIAL IDEAS WERE DETERRITORIALIZED WHICH INFLUENCED QUANTITATIVE
AND QUALITATIVE RELATIONSHIPS OF PROGRAMS, SPACE AND MATERIALITY. THE EMERGENCE OF
SEVERAL ORGANIZATIONS APPLIED TO THE MOLECULAR SCALE OF MATERIAL CONSISTENCY (GLASS,
COMPOSITE MATERIALS) AND MANIFESTED SPATIALLY AND PROGRAMMATICALLY- THROUGH, BUNCHING,
CLUSTERING, AND PLEATING.

ASSEMBLAGE

THE MALL IS AN ASSEMBLAGE OF EMERGENT QUALITATIVE BEHAVIOUR WHICH OPERATED WITHIN
THE LIMITS OF THE TECHNIQUE. THE PROGRAM, SPATIAL ORGANIZATION AND PERFORMANCE WERE
ALL INFORMED BY THE ABSTRACT MACHINE, WHICH RESULTED IN A VERY SPECIFIC YET HETROGENOUS
FORM THAT RESPONDED TO THE MULTIPLICITY OF CAPITALISM.

Notes

1. Henri Bergson, *The Creative Mind: An Introduction to Metaphysics*, Philosophical Library (New York), 1946, p 21.
2. Time is irreversible because our memory prevents us from reliving any moment. Duration, consisting of accumulated moments and experience, is also irreversible due to the same reasoning. See Bergson, *Creative Evolution*, Henry Holt (New York), 1911, pp 5-6.
3. Lines of external observations and internal experience can be seen as the convergence of lines of both objectivity and of reality. Each line defines a qualitatitve probabilism, and in their convergence they define a superior probabilism that is capable of solving problems and bringing the condition back to the real or concrete. See Bergson, *Mind-Energy*, Henry Holt (New York), 1920, pp 6-7.
4. Bergson, *The Creative Mind*, p 21.
5. Constructivism assumes that all knowledge is formed with the process of learning. Understanding is accretive. This model is based on fluctuating adaptations and transformations occurring within its system, but not limited to it. Constructivism utilises the concept of an epistemological evolution, the notion that the development of knowledge is an ongoing process. Our experiences build upon each other and consolidated together form a heterogeneous body of knowledge. This provides for us a framework for inference and for adaptation to changing conditions in our environment. The determination of our understanding is based, then,

... if one can cut out from the universe the systems for which time is only an abstraction, a relation, a number, the universe itself becomes something different. If we could grasp it in its entirety, inorganic but interwoven with organic beings, we should see it ceaselessly taking on forms as new, as original, as unforeseeable as our states of consciousness.
Henri Bergson[1]

Determinism of time as an abstraction, a number and quantity needs to shift to the nondeterminate, qualitative duration of temporality where the past, present and future are simultaneous. We take advantage of this qualitative duration by using high-end animation software where the present is bound by the past with openness towards the future. This shifts our knowledge of the objective world to one which is not fixed in space and time. Objective reality is a potential world of possibility where creative ideas intertwine with temporal animation techniques, maximising the potential for creating programmes, materials and forms that are new and original.

What is time? The determinism of Newtonian science presented an axiomatic vision of the universe, deducing empirical laws of planetary motion from the inverse-square principle, defining gravity as being an essential quality of bodies; because of his religious tendencies Newton accepted mechanically inexplicable forces. In essence, every event in nature is predictable, and predetermined by initial conditions. Like a clock that exists objectively,

independent of any beings, nature is described as a simple reduced system which is causal and can go backwards and forwards without altering its effects. Time is symmetrical because it is cyclical in motion, so one planet will have an effect on another, and past and future are interchangeable. Historical records, for instance, can read from left to right and vice versa, and any given moment assumes to be exactly like any other moment. Time here is static, where past, present and future are subjective and experientially based, rather than reflecting an ontological divide. It is a simplified standardised notational system separate from beings, a number, a reductive quantity with zero duration and an object at every moment we perceive it. Chance plays no part and unsurprisingly time, an afterthought, is reversible.

Henri Bergson among others has emphasised the difference between time as a number or static entity, and time intermingled with organic bodies. Here time has no reality independent of the subject. The dynamic view of time or temporality recognises that the future lacks the reality of the past and present, and that reality evolves as time passes. Temporality has the unity of a future which makes the present the process of having been. This is real time where we can perceive the past, present and future simultaneously, and is our being in the world or, precisely, the time in our head. Where past, present and future are never the same, time consists of duration, is qualitative and irreversible.[2]

Only when a system behaves in a sufficiently spontaneous way is there a difference between past and future, and time is qualitative, directional and irreversible. This randomness and spontaneity must outweigh causality and predictability to increase qualitative potentiality. Potentiality is indeterminate

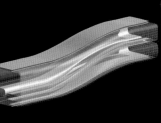

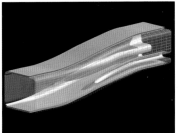

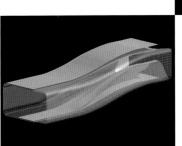

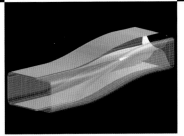

Opposite
Animation board: includes animations and analysis describing quantitative and qualitative influences.

This page
Spatial studies due to animation technique.

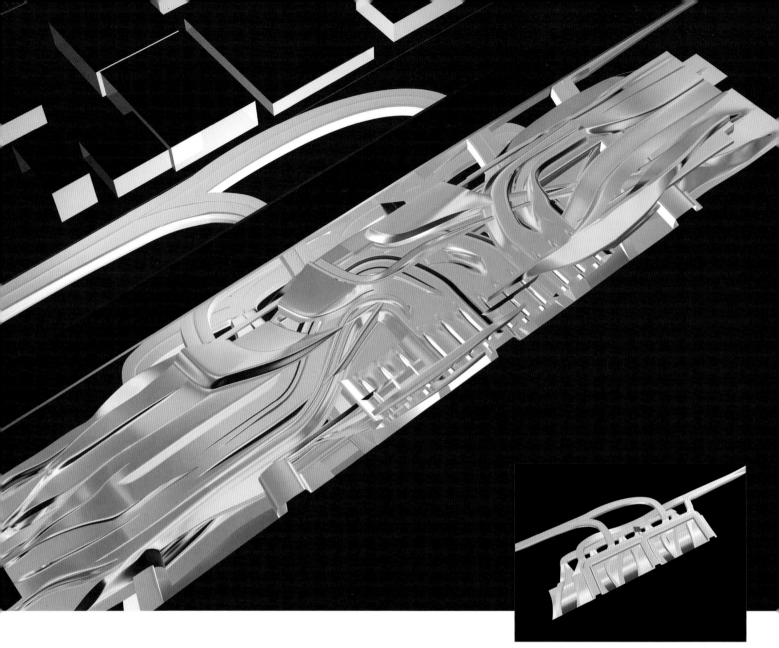

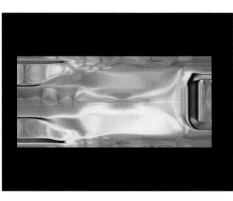

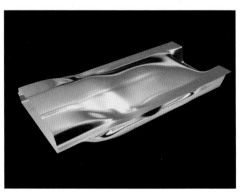

upon the indeterminacy of our experiences, and not the other way round. In this manner the constructed framework maintains unity, while being able to transform and mutate according to new conditions. The Constructivist analysis provides animation processes with an opportunity to develop creatively within a mode of abstraction. See Humberto Maturana and Francisco Varela, 'Autopoiesis and Cognition: The Realization of the Living' in *Boston Studies in the Philosophy of Science*, Robert S Cohen and Marx W Wartofsky (eds), vol 42 Dordecht (Holland): (D. Reidel Publishing Co., 1980).

6. According to the second law of thermodynamics all natural systems degenerate when left to themselves and have a tendency towards entropy. Time here is a directional continuum and cannot be reversed. This is exemplified in meteorological situations such as the development of clouds before a thunderstorm. See Norbert Weiner, *Newtonian and Bergsonian Time*, *Cybernetics: Control and*

and reliant on the actualisation of future possibility. Here time is a varying principle at each stage of division. Real time is quantifiable at precise moments of past and present, a quantitative multiplicity, and it is between these two moments, or duration, that the qualitative potentials are at their maximum. For example, in the act of choosing, we choose from a number of possibilities and cannot undo this act once we have chosen. There is an asymmetry between the past which is fixed and the future that is yet to exist. At the precise moment of selection, there is a change (bifurcation) where the potentials have moved from being at their maximum to an actualised probability. This probability describes only the potential property and not the actual physical property of objects.[3] The objective substance of materialism has disintegrated into relative potentialities instead of material realities. Thus in duration, considered as creative evolution, there is a perpetual creation of possibility and not only of reality.[4]

This qualitative duration inhabits itself in the

Communication in the Animal and Machine, MIT Press (Cambridge, Mass), 1948, p 32.

7. For more specific discussion on this double articulation, refer to my article 'Machinic Phylum: Single and Double Articulation' in Ali Rahim (ed), *Contemporary Processes in Architecture*, Architectural Design, vol 70, no 3, August 2000, pp 62–69.

8. In a dynamic system such as that of an oscillation between two trajectories, we generally find a mixture of states that makes the transition to a single point ambiguous. Dynamic systems are unstable and all regions of such systems, no matter how small, will always contain states belonging to each of the two types of trajectories. A trajectory, then, becomes unobservable, and we can only predict the statistical future of such a system. See Ilya Prigogine and Isabelle Stengers, *Order Out of Chaos: Man's New Dialogue with Nature*, Bantam Books (New York), 1984, p 264.

9. Gilles Deleuze specifically says, 'It is no longer a question of imposing a form upon a matter but of elaborating an increasingly rich [and consistent] material. ... What makes a material increasingly rich is the same as what holds heterogeneities together without their ceasing to be heterogeneous.' See Gilles Deleuze and Felix Guattari, *1000 Plateaus: Capitalism and Schizophrenia*, University of Minnesota Press, Minneapolis, 1980, p 514.

10. Ibid, p 415.

11. Instants themselves have no duration. The state of an artificial system depends on what it was at the moment immediately before. See Bergson, *Creative Evolution*, pp 21–2.

12. Alfred North Whitehead argues that there are different stages in the act of becoming conscious of potential – and that we cannot pinpoint the actual instance as temporal increments are able to be subdivided and the act is dependent upon earlier and later moments. As duration is not reducible to points or instants, we are unable to pinpoint the act.

13. What makes a form machinic is when it intermingles with bodies in society. Gilles Deleuze and Felix Guattari explain it as, 'attractions and repulsions, sympathies and antipathies, alterations, amalgamations, penetrations and expansions that effect all bodies and their relation to each other.' Op cit, p 90.

matrices of high-end animation software between the conceptualisation of the initial idea and its material form. These animations are nonlinear, endogenic and bottom-up where effects are not causal; they are no longer proportional to their causes but are unpredictable and emergent. They operate with spontaneity and develop traits simultaneously with the nonreversible directionality of temporality where the present and past are simultaneous. The future is undecided but is bound by its past and makes present the process of having been. This epistemological evolution is an ongoing process that tends to grow in an opportunistic manner and is constructive.[5] This allows it to increase in complexity, while its traits become historically bound to previous states and simultaneously develop new ones. These traits developed by gradient force-fields move far from equilibrium and material quantities and develop qualitative potentialities.

Here variation in space is temporal and actual, based on chance, and differs from key-framed animations which are determined and metaphorical. For example, a child growing in height through time, as it becomes older, is actual and hence realised potential at every stage of its development as opposed to the changing dimension of a road or statistical graph in space which is metaphorical. These key-framed animations spatialise time and deny the reality of temporal 'becoming'.

The efficacy of these temporal animations works in one direction in time, since future events cannot influence past events if played in reverse. If we were to play in reverse a video showing the turbulence of clouds before a thunderstorm we would see downdraughts when we expect updraughts, turbulence growing coarser rather than finer in texture, lightning preceding instead of following the changes of cloud and so on.[6] Irreversible time is necessary for temporality. For example, if we used a time-lapse video to capture planets moving and played it backwards, it would look the same due to the progression of movements being the same, with the only difference being that the planets were moving in reverse. This system still operates within the Newtonian universe and is not unlike key-framed animations, in which the effects of changes and deformations are reversible and thus predictable.

Temporal animations without key-frames are reliant on a double articulation of content, or concepts, and expression which is its specific corollary or technique. Content is comprised of unformed matter or intensities that are destabilising forces or potentials, while technique is the embodiment of precise combinations, influenced and shaped within the animation, that serve as tensors or functions and are temporal. The potential (the forces) destabilises technique and opens it up to new associations[7] through time. To be able to develop techniques that correspond to concepts, we need to understand concepts through their limits; limits[8] are defined by the probabilities of potentials. In this manner, techniques do not restrain or limit potentials, but rather the probabilities of potentials limit and guide how techniques are organised. This series of procedures and combinations are adaptive and reliant on each other's arrangements explored through an iterative process. The concept informs the technique, and vice versa.[9] This retains distinction within the animation, because distinction subsists, and recreates traits or potential. The simultaneous relationship of concept and technique, although distinct, is affected by continuous variation. These elements behave in unison as quanta of single flow.[10]

Within this singular flow animation of content and expression, spontaneous organisations emerge at differing points within the animation.

Within this singular flow animation of content and expression, spontaneous organisations emerge at differing points within the animation – they have no scale or objectified time and are a double articulation that results in an abstract machine. This machine maximises generative potential that is simultaneously real but not concrete. It refers to the infinite machineness of a temporal organism, a machine with every piece machined to an infinite degree. This exceeds any mechanical process and maximises qualitative flows of potential in duration represented by the animation's interactions between its parts. It is a synthesis of unity and multiplicity of potentials understood through duration. In other words, if an object is a type of numerical multiplicity, it marks specific points or instants[11] that demarcate the duration when qualitative multiplicity occurs. Qualitative multiplicities are indivisible quantitatively without a change in nature, because of their unequal differences distributed in real time. Within this self-organised machine, the potentials are not projected and their possibilities are limitless.

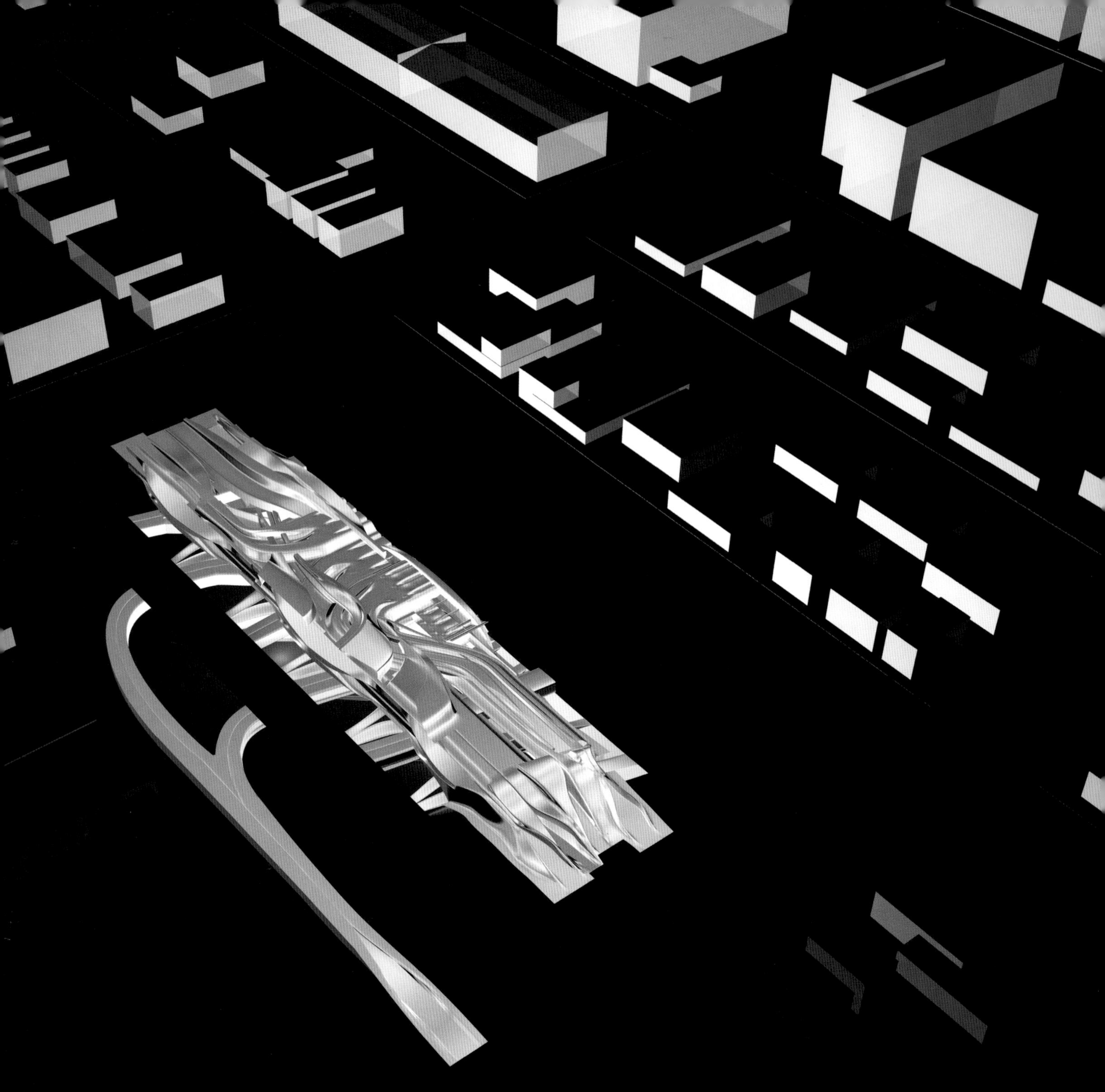

Previous spread:
Left top
Axonometric view of project.

Inset top
Detail of infrastructure in
axonometric view.

Inset middle
Detail of theatre in plan view.

Inset bottom
Detail of theatre in perspective
view.

This spread:
Above
Perspective view of project
on site.

Opposite top
Perspective view of offices.

Opposite bottom
Perspective view of project.

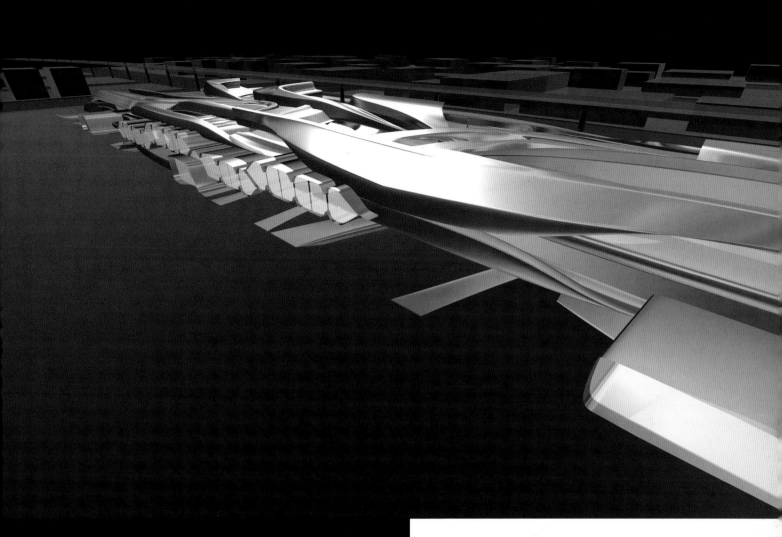

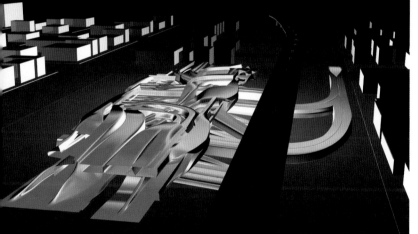

Credits:
Project title: Confluence
of Commerce, South Asia.
Principal: Ali Rahim. Design
Research Assistants:
John Cooney, Brian Kimura,
Lee Rubenstein. Assistant:
Nathaniel Hadley.
Irreducible Time:
Machining Possibilities
Research Assistant:
Anne Kojima. Academic
Support from the Department
of Architecture, University
of Pennsylvania.

Our perception of this duration is a projection of actuality, and this represents a potential for something actual, as opposed to something actual. This projection now is singular and when projected points in one direction, instead of multiple directions dependent on when we are conscious of it.[12] In other words, when the potentials have emerged into an abstract machine they are temporally actualised through the differentiation of potential. This process of actualisation is the flow from one state to another. This multiplicity is projected into the material world where programmes, material and form are actualised from a qualitative state of potentials to a machinic organisation.[13] This specific organisation of nonisotropic programme, materials and forms still maintains real time as an irreversible flow where variation in space is temporal and actual – it has realised its potential at every stage of development.

Determinate materialism of time as a number, and of reversible time, needs to shift to nondeterminate, nonreversible temporality, which has the unity of a future that makes present the process of having been. This qualitative duration between past and future maximises generative potentials within the framework of nonlinear, bottom-up animation techniques, and meets the objective world as actual machined forms of architecture that are innovative, flexible in use yet precise. ∆

Animated
Bodies

Kas Oosterhuis, the principal of Oosterhuis.nl and Professor at the Technical University Delft overseeing the Research Programme Hyperbody (www.hyperbody.nl), describes how 'technology is turning wild'. Its invasion by digital animation techniques at the design stage is only the start, with the once-static architectural body set to become 'animated bodies'. This futuristic vision comes to life in Oosterhuis's new Trans-ports project — a programmable vehicle with interacting skin.

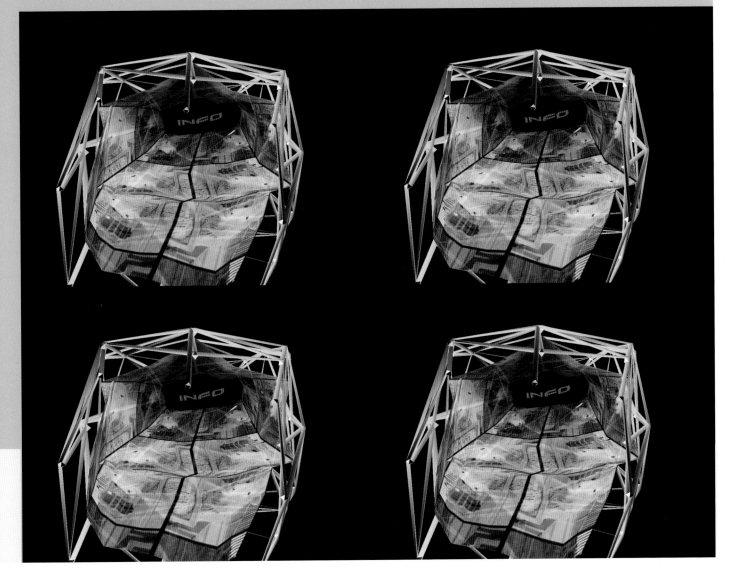

Let us take a close look at the configurations that real-time constructions can assume and the climates that the real-time conditioned environments can take on. The invasion of intuition, emotion and unpredictability into the design process, and subsequently into the behaviour of structures, is now in full swing thanks to the electronic revolution. The buildings that are being constructed today are no longer the final stage of our yearning for control. The real-time processes, the bottom-up networks are in principle out of control. Never again will a single individual (the architect) be able to cherish the illusion of having a process fully under control. In a reverse of domestication, building is going wild. The atmospheres created by climate installations will no longer be designed to form a stable, ideal climate; on the contrary, the atmospheres will tend to become unpredictable, influenced by real and virtual users, run by scripts that draw their information from databases. The interior climate, image, sound – and even the physical, visible form of the architecture – will be dynamic elements that actively become a part of a global push-and-pull network. In Philip Kerr's thriller *Gridiron* (1995), a computer game played by the architect's son becomes lodged in the database of the operating system of a building – described as an extreme version of Norman Foster's Shanghai Bank – which turns into a pitiless killing machine.

The architect will increasingly need a well-trained intuitive insight into the possibilities of operating complex processes. It is thus highly appropriate to regard the computer as an instrument, like a pet that must be tamed and bred. The computer as pet offers both discipline and unpredictable behaviour in the design process, and we architects must become intuitive about the behaviour of computer-driven design systems and the mathematics behind them. However, the pet will never posses human intelligence because the computer does not develop to match this.

How can we be so arrogant as to believe that? While

people think with the relatively slow speed of chemical processes, the computer processes information at the speed of light. In many respects it is far faster than the human brain. A serious common mistake is to suppose that the computer will never develop the same kind of consciousness and insight as humans. I think it might eventually simulate insight of that kind in order to be able to communicate with people, to please us. It could develop a consciousness of its own, linked to millions of other computers in a universal network, and the results of this development would eventually be uncontrollable by humans.

Once digital technology invades the building body, that body will never be the same again. Technology evolves at a fast rate, far beyond the speed of carbon-based evolution. It uses our human bodies as software for its technological bodies – just think of the car, using its driver as software to travel along a route. In the meantime it has become clear that human development is not the final goal of evolution, and that technology is gradually taking over our prominent position. What were initially technological extensions of the human body, to increase our power, are now moving step by step towards becoming complex emotional instruments whose behaviour is unpredictable.

Technology is turning wild. Once it invades

the design material in the design process and animates it in real time it will become unstoppable, not only at the design stage but also afterwards in the life cycle of the project. This is where animate form turns into animate body. Architectural bodies will be literally animated. Architecture no longer has a desire to withstand mobile forces; its visible form is now becoming as unpredictable as the weather. Architecture is turning wild.

Trans-ports

Trans-ports is a programmable vehicle which connects the virtual and the real ... trans-ports is a data-driven, supple structure which changes shape and content in real time ... this active structure is the first building of its kind that generates constructive strength when needed and relaxes when mobile forces are modest ... trans-ports is physically driven by computer-controlled pistons that operate in a coordinated fashion like a distributed swarm of filaments in a muscular bundle ... of content ... the flexible electronic skin follows the movments of the data-driven structure ... the skin is not a one-way display of information but interacts with the users in a two-way exchange ... trans-ports is a push-and-pull medium ... it offers valuable broadcast time to its shareholders on a time-sharing basis ... individual and collective interaction creates a new bond between architecture and its users ... when technique digs itself deep into the building body, that form becomes animated in real time ... architecture goes wild. ⌂

Above
Pneumatic structure.

Opposite top
Animated skin.

Opposite middle
Game mode.

Opposite bottom
Interactive media flows.

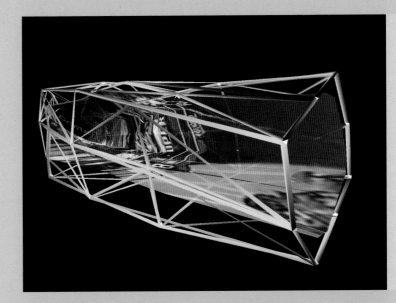

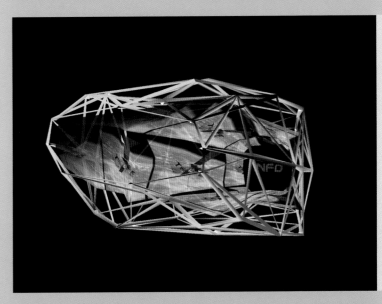

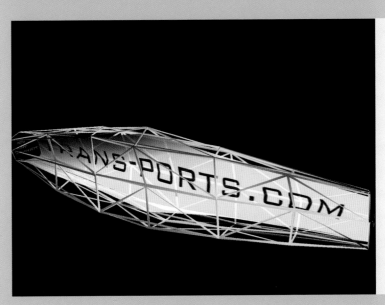

Christopher Romero's hybrid
constructions integrate computational
and physical environments with a
range of media components, content
and subject matter to create an
engaging participatory experience
for the visitor.

The Clearing

Here, he presents an issue of
The Clearing, a 'compressed' document
with scenes from 'Ghost Stories', 'The
Captor' and 'Poppethead', all produced
as installations for public exhibition.

The Clearing

(Awakenings and Meditations)

christopher romero

The Clearing (Frag Text)

animate
god animated the dust (arouse latent liveliness)

animated puppets
mechanical objects that appear to move as real ones do

clearing
an opening, cut or split that alters perception

zest
extremely alive and/or broken

arouse
I am filled with breath and aroused

animatism
attribution of consciousness to inanimate objects

authentic (scale, density, meaning)
bigness / smallness / weightless / lifeless

actual (representation)
it looks so real – it must be real

stimulation (through simulation)
C:\animate\behaviours\aggressive\attract ...

presence
encapsulate the presence of other and self
within the 'system'

snapshot
sampled image, sampled time, fragmented
hard drive, disconnection from experience

based on a true story
it has so much weight in the mind, it is potentially
much more painful that way

intermediate surface
viewport, portal, fissure, lens, widow's walk

awake (sleepless)
not because you want to be, but because it takes
up so much time and there is only enough for
a few more years

habit
don't start there again, it is the same place
as before – start here instead

making (and unmaking) space
memory production factory

Scenes

1. 'Ghost Stories'
Animation as applied material (visual and auditory fabric
within, upon, around, a physical environment) =
enhancement + application of narrative

2. 'The Captor'
Animation of an aggressive and dynamic system (implied
dimensional and behavioural space – cyberspace as a spatial
metaphor) = illusion + procedure

3. 'Poppethead'
Animation as part of a physical/digital hybrid system (physical
computing with variable feedback) = manipulation + control

Ghost Stories

relive
he took pleasure in tasting the experience again
and again

prayer
a petition to the salt of the earth

fireside chats
explosion! fire blows out – embers land in stream –
sudden burning and blindness

wishing well
ponderance, desire, longing

travel log
documentation of one's experience while travelling –
hyperaware of difference

invisibility of sleep
accountability for the crimes committed in dreams

text illuminations
generation and mutation of form, space and event –
metamorphosis of transient mental image

me
I see myself everywhere

mourning
she never got over her feelings of loss and the
inevitability of her own mortality

absence 1
extreme presence

memory machine
that terrible machine collects far too much information
– I never want to know that much about myself

heaviness
power and might – an expression of connectedness

salt screen
diluted earth – organic substance

vast
oh how we long for the openness of the West

surface mutation
musical form and the interplay of imagery applied to a
seemingly still surface

Details

The installation is comprised of a 12–16 foot metal shed. The framing
is exposed on the exterior of the structure and galvanised-metal
siding lines the interior of the space inverting the relationship
between inside and outside. Once inside the structure, the ambient
sound is that of a thunderstorm intermixed with a range of sound
events and auditory environments. Centrally located in the space is
a square 'screen', on the wooden floor of the space, which is created
by pouring salt onto the surface. The projection from above points
at this transient surface and spatially creates an image not unlike
a reflecting pool or wishing well, around which four small wooden
cubes are situated. These 'staging' elements reveal the participatory
nature of the space. The audience becomes part of the structure
of the piece. The projection rotates 90 degrees every 24 seconds
so that the orientation of the space itself changes repeatedly.

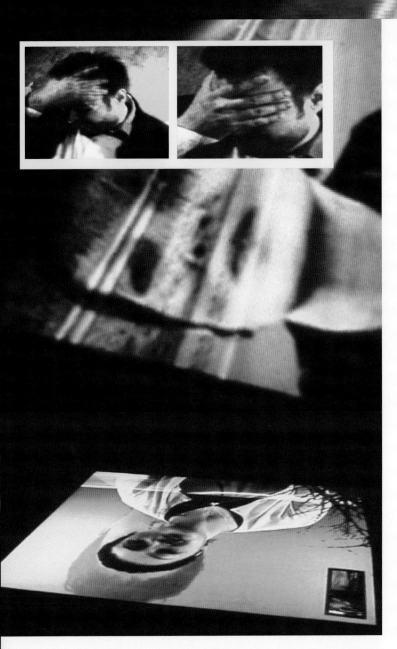

Ghost Stories (cont.)

character(s)
a representation, often heavily manipulated for
the sake of content, form and narrative

gesture (awk)
captured and processed chance

erasable
hubble telescope (relational shift)

thunderstorm
inverted structure – turbulence

skin
shelter/cathedral/decay

country western
I remember endless highways and AM radio.
I see road maps with memories pencilled in of all
those who stayed behind and our long goodbyes.

drama
lightning and thunder are dramatic – particularly
on the open road or alone in a squeaky old house
or when you are filled with deep sadness

organic
even organically derived foods have been enhanced
by technology – that is how they remain so pure
and wholesome

deafening silence
the space has been enclosed by the absence
of noise – it is loud and penetrating

rattle
the thunder rattles, or rattlesnake
(American West context)

tranquillity
candlelight and burning wood

time reversal
longing, hesitation, remorse, nostalgia

Details

Within the central floor projection, 60 'characters' are presented
for 20 seconds each. These 'scenes' are composed with many layers
of applied imagery and ironic decontextualised expressions and
gestures. The character is captured in a state of change and is often
caught in an uncomfortable loop. The awkward movements of the
body and the tortured facial expressions create an experience for the
viewer that is incredibly organic and abrupt. The viewer is further
pulled into the scenes through the sound environment that is at once
meditative, ambient, disconnected and obtuse.

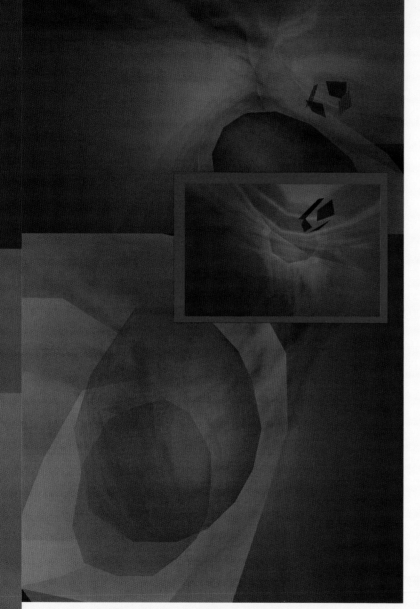

The Captor

wound
scattered in digital flesh

speed
system variables / bandwidth + processor

time deficiency
absence of now – making plans, making plans, try simulation

spy
I am a spy in your world – a code warrior – my word is truth

solitude
black widows live in the woodpile

psychological void
openings that clear room for new ideas –
new images – new relationships to others

internalising fear
you have no control over the system

desire
all the children have red wagons – Xavier would
like to have one too, and stuff to put inside

voyeur
networked connectivity – primary content

everything(ness)
drifting through nothingness with certain yet
unbearable desire

special
not everyone is special – it is a lie

emptiness
once you realise that you are not special

dynamic aggregate
mutation of the system – v|spin cycle discloses
atmospheric signs of change

madness
intense density of experience may cause
several forms of madness, see clearing

escape
… from what you want (and/or) … from what
is imposed upon you

position (drift)
here is not a constant (cities within cities)

Details

This sequence of screen captures helps to illustrate the changing
characteristics of the overall environment within 'The Captor'.
The sound environment droanes awkwardly as the 'dynamic
aggregates' and colour cells of the system move chaotically around
the visitor. The 'centre' of the system holds four reference panels.
Each panel emphasises aspects of one's state of mind when
entering the space – attempting to make 'sense' of it all.
The atmosphere changes colour constantly, and the rate of change
in the environment is in a constant state of flux. It is almost
impossible to orient oneself in the space – it becomes effectively
spaceless.

The Captor (cont.)

surrender
... your position in the system – you will not be released – you are a captive

captive
your imagination has been hindered by 'all that is possible'

absence 2
extreme density of one's inner self, see solitude

accident
they were hit at over 70 mph by a large Continental – they went off the bridge never knowing what hit them – crash!

loss of inscription
all visible signs of memory had been 'written over' – they were no longer human

fracture
self-criticism – a generative model within the superstructure

abruptness
collisions and flash links (stitched fabric)

intimacy
suitable to encourage the telling of secrets

fabric of the system
perimeter blur, elasticity of controls, alternate mapping, drift, gravitational shift, particle dynamic, composites, hybrids, transformative behaviours, atmospheric density, transparency, areas of saturated experience

invisibility
Alijandro walked to the door – a portal between worlds – and jumped. At that instant it appeared as though he had never left at all. The scars were more visible to his sisters and brothers. It was so obvious that something was wrong.

Details

This quality of being nowhere has a strong impact on the captives of the system. An insurmountable feeling of anxiety overwhelms those who fight to find balance, continuity, cohesiveness and control. Only those captives who purge this anxiety may feel a sense of calm as they are inevitably consumed.

The images seen above do not appropriately represent the aforementioned experience. These images are captured artefacts from a privileged viewpoint. The captive would never experience these scenes as they have been displayed above with such visual and spatial clarity. One must imagine being engulfed in a visual, auditory and atmospheric chaos with no way out.

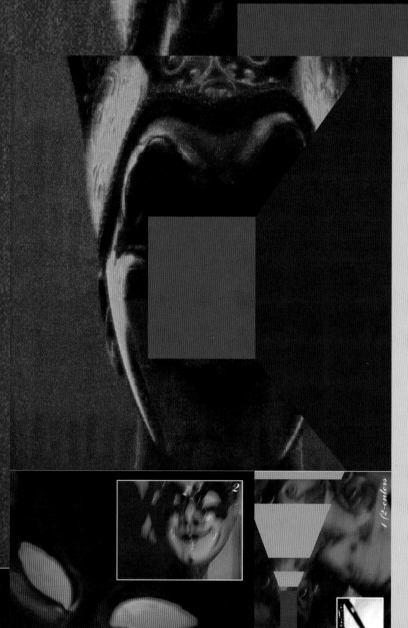

Poppethead

animated form 1
a sequence and/or series of events that are altered by input mechanisms

animated form 2
a structural device that causes individuals to take action – altering the local 'scene'

character mutation
Gregor became the murderer he had been reading about in the morning newspaper

marionette
a disjointed puppet (manipulated from above) whose behaviour is determined by the will of others

replica
a copied experience leading to confusion or misunderstandings of the self

carnival
a travelling amusement environment usually including sideshows and space/time modulators

ugliness
lack of difference (addiction)

hidden gesture
playing dead – the puppet is not breathing

machine 1
a device used to produce an effect especially as a mechanical and visual means of luring a visitor to participate within a system of control (trick)

machine 2
a system or device (computer) that insists that a performance of a human task must be completed

tactic
an artist's manoeuvre or operative

control
step 1 – glowing images (attractor)
step 2 – restraining device (curiosity)

fear
a state marked by feelings of agitation and/or anxiety

body scanning
the body and its orientation to the world can be altered through sensory manipulation, see torture

Details

'Poppethead' is an installation sited physically at the centre of a broad darkened space. From a distance, a visitor sees the curious image of cables and flickering monitors hanging from the large wooden beams of a puppeteer's cruciform guides. This hybrid construction hangs from a dark invisible place far above the floor level. 'Poppethead' operates at many levels as a manipulator and system of trickery and control. To the participant, the piece is an awkward device for 'interacting' with a visual and auditory narrative. The scenes build, based on simple input triggers placed within four mechanical sleds beneath the hanging monitor tubes. These scenes vary depending on the number of participants within the piece.

Poppethead (cont.)
enter 1, jump 2, jump 3, jump 4
narrative structure input log (shift, shift ...)

truncate
a staging device employed to disorient a viewer through
abrupt manipulation of points of reference

cruciform
parti-diagram = dehumaniser

operatic form
created with set pieces such as solos, duets, trios,
quartets, etc, all designed to dramatise the interaction
with a machine and fool the participant into achieving
an unreachable goal

umbilical cord
the flexible cord-like structure connecting an 'individual'
to a means of nourishment (cathode-ray projection
stream, network terminal)

leash
a chain, rope, strap or cable attached to a harness
of 'the animal' esp. human – used to lead it, hold it
or drag it

simple
it is a simple trick – but I will see for myself –
stand back

devil
an energetic, mischievous, daring, clever person,
device or machine, especially one having teeth or
spikes and used for tearing at one's expectations

fool
one who has been tricked and/or made to appear
ridiculous = participant

wounded vision
a paralysis caused by image(s) [image addiction
paralysis]

Details
To visitors, the overall image of the scene is too much to bear.
Curiosity about the 'content' of the piece with its glowing images and
echoing sounds beneath the structure overpowers any apprehension.
But once they participate and become part of the 'machine' they are
effectively killed. Any potential interaction was a farce. Each
participant now lies lifeless beneath the monitors' light – suspended
in a continuous looping narrative.

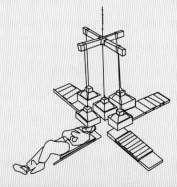

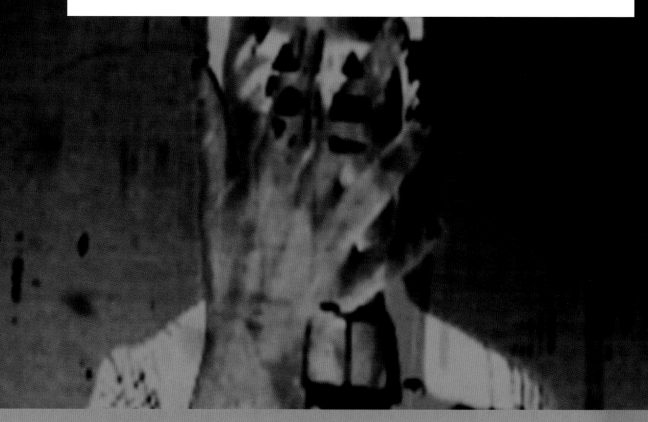

The Clearing
Notes

'Ghost Stories' is a multimedia installation piece that integrates a physical structure, a sound environment and a number of visual components and staging elements to create a completely immersive experience for the visitor. This installation engages an ongoing preoccupation with dislocation, psychological voids, memory, loss and chance. The idea of 'ghost stories' is one of transient thoughts, experiences, relationships and aspects of human interaction and expression that become caught between organic substance, the space of personal memory and a state of emotional catharsis and empathy. This piece creates a place for reflection and for projection of the self through an assemblage of sound and image events within a physical construction in which the audience becomes a completely integrated centre of this hybrid architecture.

Within this piece, a visitor assumes an essential role as a participant in the spatial construction of the work. Unlike in many computer-based 'interactive' works, the aspect of 'presence' is of the utmost importance in that the physical relationship of the visitor in the turbulent inverted form of the metal shed helps to characterise the irony of the 'staged' environment with its auditory, visual and structural components. An individual assumes a certain posture within the scene (while seated on one of the four central stools in the space), not unlike sitting around a camp fire or the position of thoughtful repose when someone is looking into a wishing well. The 'transient' salt screen further breaks the continuity of the experience of the visual material by presenting the likelihood of change and fragmentation. The central visual and auditory experience, with participants seated around the floor projection, creates an intriguing peripheral experience for those who remain outside the central space. Their experience is animated by isolated sound events that are accessed through small speakers inside tin cans hanging from the side walls of the corrugated metal enclosure.

'The Captor' was created as part of an ongoing exhibition, The Second World Exhibition, curated by Alternet Fabric and Canal+ in Lausanne and Paris. A small group of architects, designers and artists were invited to 'install' work in a virtual museum space, creating a combined extendible environment on the shared network of the Internet. Each of the participants was given specific guidelines for building the shared environment in VRML in order that there might be a controlled organisational structure in place for accessing, navigating, experiencing and exiting the work.

'The Captor' is a living digital system that has an existence without the presence of the 'museum' visitor. In other words, the space has behavioural characteristics that do not rely on a visitor's input or navigation. For the visitor (captive), the experience is abrupt, disorienting, chaotic and frightening. The system is in control of the visitor who finds it almost impossible to gain any sense of control to exit the environment. 'The Captor' is a controlling, progressive, computational system. It is a project that illustrates the idea of losing control of 'enabling' technologies.

'Poppethead' is an installation piece that engages man's addiction to images, technological devices and the idea of captured or intercepted experiences. A visitor to the space in which 'Poppethead' hangs sees a strange assemblage of mechanical sleds, video cables and the glowing – often pulsating – image of five floating computer monitors. The assemblage hovers above the floor, a mere 18 inches from the surface of the sleds below. The piece is suspended by a large wooden cruciform structure that mimics the proportions and orientation of a marionette's 'guides'.

The visitor becomes a participant by lying down on the floor and sliding underneath one of the four character screens. By sliding under the system the participant engages a trigger that initiates a visual and auditory sequence. Formally, the participant has now completed a quadrant of the overall 'composition'. Conceptually, the participant has effectively 'killed' any proactive interaction since he or she is now a mere puppet in the machine. When additional participants in the open space submit themselves to the machine the character scene shifts, representing the additional character in the overall act.

From the outside the audience sees the ironic scene created by the lifeless bodies beneath the assemblage of technology. The participants are controlled by the device. They complete the circuits. They blindly enter into the literal manipulation of their own bodies and willingly participate in their own objectification. Staring at the screens and interacting only passively, the participants become completely lifeless – mechanised and dehumanised. Necessarily, the only thing seen by the observer – the visitor outside the machines' grip – is an oddity; an object of control and death. The images on the screens themselves can only be seen from below – therefore, from within the system. This is the trap: the anxiety and power of one's own curiosity and submission to the power of the unseen image.

All contents: © 1999, 2000 Christopher Romero.
Additional credits: Marc Alt - production, development and authoring assistant on 'Ghost Stories; Winston Yang - programming, production and design assistant on 'The Captor'.

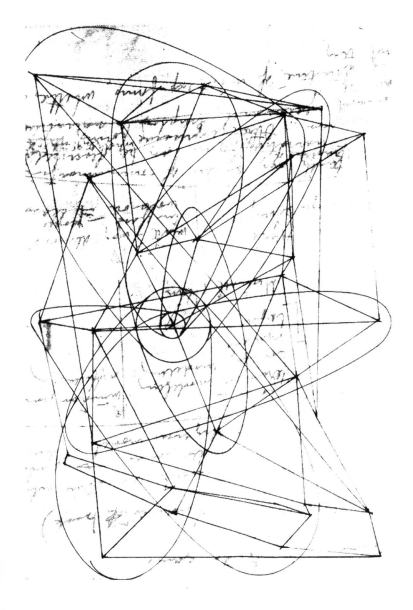

Broadcast Interface, Los Angeles

As a member of the design faculty at SCI-Arc and a partner in Durfee Regn Sandhaus – a multidisciplinary design studio that produces digital interfaces, exhibitions and architecture – Tim Durfee is working outside the conventional confines of architecture as a discipline. Here he describes how, in a project for a CD-ROM magazine, he has put to use his knowledge of the organisational, scenic and spatial qualities of the city.

Great economic and technological convergences are redefining all forms of media. Television, radio and personal computers are merging or, in some cases, becoming merely different instruments for receiving identical content.

Currently, however, these forms of communication remain unevolved to operate in any integrated way. Because of this, new modalities for structuring and accessing content could be developed that are flexible, hybrid and, most importantly, can be experienced both linearly and nonlinearly.

Cities provide useful models for developing this kind of information infrastructure. Content is zoned, planned and parcelled. Places of information are visited by audiences using their TV or radio, or by surfing the Web with a computer (until the appliances themselves also merge completely).

Like real cities, these urbanised clusters of information are spatial, nested and complex. As spaces, however, they are critically different from those associated with current forms of media. The environments in film, television, video games and many Web and software interfaces are typically products of scenic design, for which the goal is the illusionistic evocation of real places to serve a narrative. Even nonfiction pieces for film or televised broadcast use lifelike environments as typological cues to inspire specific emotional responses, such as trust (for news programmes) or desire (for advertising). With the evolution of purely linear forms such as television and radio, space can be conceived of as a performative matrix for structuring information, rather than as a strictly pictorial context for narrative. (This is, of course, mostly relevant for forms of content other than location-specific narrative.) The space and the elements that define it are determined by the nature and organisation

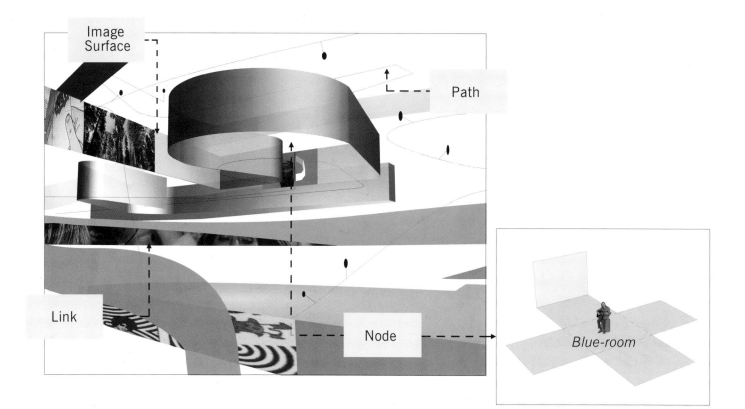

Image Surface

Path

Link

Node

Blue-room

Top and centre
Form is dictated by the paths
of the cameras. Image: ski
slopes, off season.

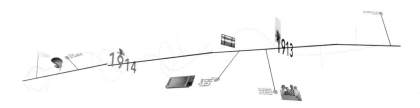

Above
Proposed interface for digital
time-line at Los Angeles
County Museum of Art.
Durfee Regn Sandhaus, 2000.

of the information itself, rather than by metaphorical references to physical structure. This concept lends itself most obviously to the design of three-dimensional digital interfaces, which can use space to make sense of complex data and enable a more spatially intuitive, less text-driven form of communication.

This project examines the applicability of principles for a purely digital, interactive architecture in a context that spans several forms of media. The client, producers of a popular CD-ROM magazine, wished to expand their programming onto television and the Web. The specific task was to develop a virtual city to be the context for the weekly music and entertainment television programme and the eventual website. The monthly CD-ROM already used a city as an organisational metaphor for its content.

The digital city was designed according to these guidelines:
1. Develop an overall structure based on the organisation of the content. [as shown above]
The city plan emerges through a process of plotting nodes where different parts of the show, such as interviews, performances, reviews and features, take place. Camera paths thread between nodes to allow for flexibility in the sequencing of the show's parts. These camera paths define the fabric of the city.
2. Develop a language of form that corresponds to the performative characteristics of the environment and pursues a condition of authenticity with the medium itself.

Specifically:

+ Avoid real-world metaphors. Walls, for example, only need to be two-dimensional – they exist to carry images and define locations.

+ Privilege the organisation of content, the definition of specific places, and the requirements of viewing data as engines of form.

+ Reveal, whenever possible, the 'mechanism' of the animation software – cameras, paths, lights, key-frames.

+ Because images, graphics, text, colour and sound have identical value in real space as in virtual space, these can be considered the truest building components in virtual space.

3. Develop one virtual site to be shared by all media.

The CD-ROM, the website and the television programme all exist in the same digital city. The experience of browsing the CD-ROM or gazing at the TV or surfing around the website differs only in the respective instruments of viewing.

4. Allow the city to grow over time.

Accretion of new camera paths, lighting, content and advertising from all three media cause the city to become more expansive and dense with each episode and each new season.

5. Incorporate a dynamic modulation of detail that corresponds to scalar shifts.

Because the programme has live people – hosts and guests – more referential, anthropomorphic elements are present when they are on screen.

This detail, however, only appears at microscales, as opposed to the larger 'urban' scales at which only more diagrammatic, 'info-morphic' elements are visible.

6. Establish continuity of form and space.

In the opening sequence, for example, the camera flies through the streets, passing locations where different events will take place at the exact time that the voice-over announces that event (as a preview of what will appear in the episode). The host is present at the node where the camera stops. After the introduction, the camera moves through the street to another node for the next part of the programme. Before a commercial break, the camera pulls away from the live people keyed into a node, flies back into the street and into an image displaying the sponsor's product (like a billboard). After the commercial break, the camera returns to the city from the same location, never breaking continuity.

Continuity is important to maintain faith in the structural predictability of the system – rather than relying on an illusion of real time, with edited, discontinuous shots. Within the city are all the elements necessary to deliver the content for all audiences (TV, CD-ROM and the Web). This immediacy collapses the temporal and geographical distance associated with televised broadcast. By applying architecture, rather than stagecraft, as the procedural medium to address the needs of effects of the content, the environment – in a way we recognize from software interfaces – becomes 'real', not referential. ᴐ

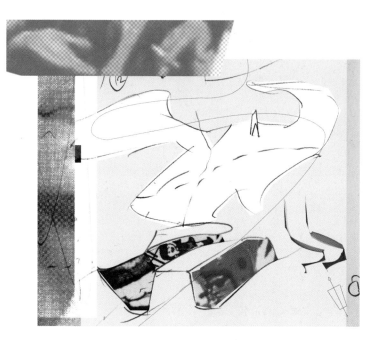

Above
'Experience' studies.

Above
The production uses virtual-set technology, for which all live hosts and guests are filmed in a blue room with the background model keyed into the background in real time. The 3-D environment shifts orientation to match all changes of the camera: position, depth of field, focus, zoom.

SCI-Arc Enterprise

'Technology is rooted in the past. It dominates the present and tends into the future. It is a real historical movement.'[1] Mies van der Rohe, 1950

The graduate and undergraduate design studios that Tim Durfee and Terry Surjan teach at SCI-Arc in Los Angeles make a strong use of digital technologies. In line with this, students are encouraged to seek out strategies that examine the role of architecture in the current social and technological landscape, and tactics for creating specific architectural responses. The profoundly scalable nature of software makes it a medium well suited to bridging these macro- and micro-orders. Much of the studios' coursework pursues a prevailing interest in viewing digital tools as vehicles to address not only the techniques of construction but also, in Paul Virilio's terms, the 'construction of technique' – that is, the rebuilding of architectural and spatial perception necessitated by ever-evolving contemporary conditions. The work presented here from various studios at SCI-Arc are evidence of this construction in process.

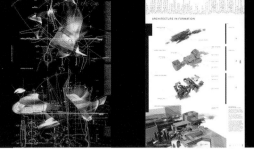

computer technologies: client/server systems; simulation/immersion/HCI (human-computer interface); and 3D engines/real-time rendering. This middleware strategy for developing MuCADEs (multi-user-computer-aided-design-environments) is a multiplatform, 3D real-time rendered environment that allows multiuser logins (avatars) to construct, communicate and navigate. The environment promotes social interaction, education and creativity.

Library for Humans and Machines

The information age marks a significant turning point in the history of the library. A new conception of matter, energy and information brought on by developments in the fields of biology, chaotic/complex-systems sciences, computation (most notably artificial intelligence and artificial life) and philosophy is transforming the way we look at the world, and consequently redefining the role the library of the future will play. In this new perspective, information is founded on a biological paradigm in which new information is revealed through the recombination and juxtaposition of existing forms of knowledge, and through the multiplication of points of view. By crossing a repository for machine learning with a hybrid library, convention centre and hotel complex on the site of a major US airport, the proposed library seeks to amplify the processes which create knowledge and induce events which invest both the physical and virtual worlds with new value.

Nine versions of the system were developed, each founded on the same basic model but with modified mapping functions. Each system was run multiple times and the output was evaluated for artefacts which had architectural potential. The proto-architectonic artefacts were then superimposed on each other in the site, and the spatial/geometric/programmatic conflicts negotiated and resolved manually.

The system was programmed in Pascal. The geometry was generated in AutoCAD and rendered in Form Z.

Animat_CGX.MOV

Using the capabilities of the modelling and animation software Maya, this project examines techniques for fluidly developing architectural responses to a site through a nonlinear process of analysis and formal research based on a variety of programmatic and environmental forces. Rather than the structurally realised building emerging at the end of the process, components are developed that transform throughout the design research according to the evolution of a

Notes
1. Mies van der Rohe,
Philip C Johnson,
The Museum of Modern Art,
(New York), 1953, second
edition.

Prisoner's Dilemma

Architectural form is a manifestation of the negotiation between multiple internal and external forces which, at large, is a collaborative process. With the tools that are available today, this project attempts to develop an intrinsically cohesive process of autopoiesis such that the 'architect' rather than the 'Architect' becomes a facilitator/moderator of these artificial/natural processes. To simulate this confluent condition, the prisoner's dilemma – a programmatic approach to understanding the intricate nature of 'non-zero sum' games and evolution through collaboration – is utilised. A process is developed so that when this 'game' is played the result will take on a three-dimensional proto-architectural form.

Middleware Strategies for MuCADEs

This project researches current technologies in CAD (computer-aided design), MUVEs (multi-user-virtual-environments) and MUDs (multi-user-domains/dungeons). It also develops middleware strategies for implementing these technologies into a design process, augmenting the range of capabilities of education and professional practice.

PlatForm combines three aspects of a design process. Human communication; information visualisation; and context with three respective

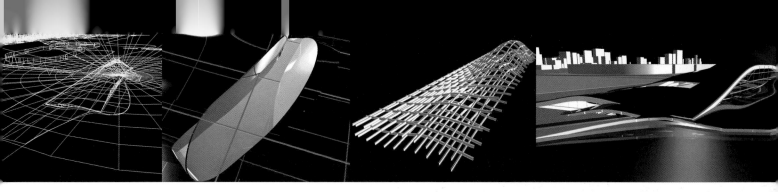

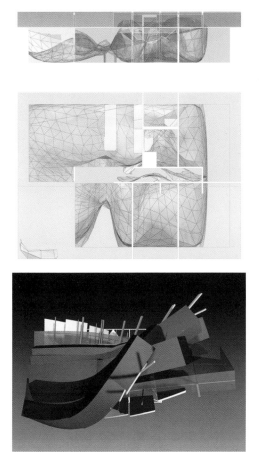

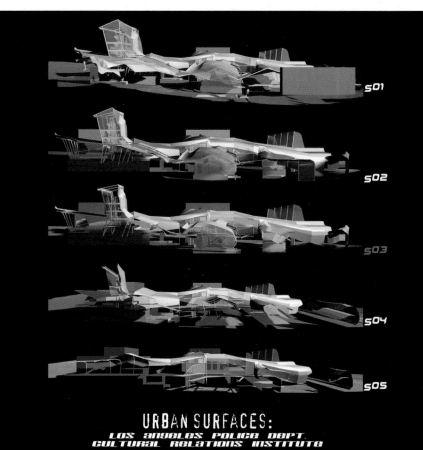

URBAN SURFACES:
LOS ANGELES POLICE DEPT.
CULTURAL RELATIONS INSTITUTE

series of control-models – each corresponding to a different site or program-related force.

Adaptive Subdivision
The goal of the studio is to establish an evolutionary architectural model (prototype) by structuring interactions within the computer and physical models that allow us to minimise our influence on its tectonic development.

We may assimilate information on occupation and time through the rereading of signs or clues. Though clues exist with or without our interaction, it is our task to interpret that which breathes life into the indexical clues. Traces of architecture already exist within the ordinary fragments strewn throughout suburban and urban landscapes; they are simply waiting to be decoded.

Spatio-temporal Imaging and Modelling
In this course students are asked to confront issues relative to the conceptualisation, visualisation and fabrication of architectural space.

The course takes the position that architecture is inseparable from its attendant modes of graphic representation; and that the particularities of each mode, or drawing convention, is by default an active agent in the architectural process. In other words, the way architecture is visualised and represented has a latent but pervasive influence on the nature of the architecture that is being developed.

Urban Surfaces
The programme is for a cultural relations institute for the Los Angeles Police Department, sited on an abandoned piece of land that overlaps several gang territories in Los Angeles, just east of MacArthur Park. The project explores the notion of 'urban surfaces' – employing architectural programmatic elements to recharge an existing topography and to act as a formal and programmatic mediator between the proposed programme and the social conditions embedded in the site. The plan view shows these urban surfaces blanketing the existing undulating topography, with the site's elevations superimposed over the image. ⚙

This page top, left to right
Byron Terrell
Animat _CGX.MOV
Thesis advisor: Tim Durfee

Centre left
Yamil Tamayo
Event model of suburban house (1966 Maverick).
Instructor: Terry Surjan

Bottom left
Robb Walker
Spatial studies: virtual model.
Instructors: Mitchell DeJarnett/Terry Surjan

Bottom right
Ken Ho
Urban Surfaces
Studio Instructor: Mitchell De Jarnett

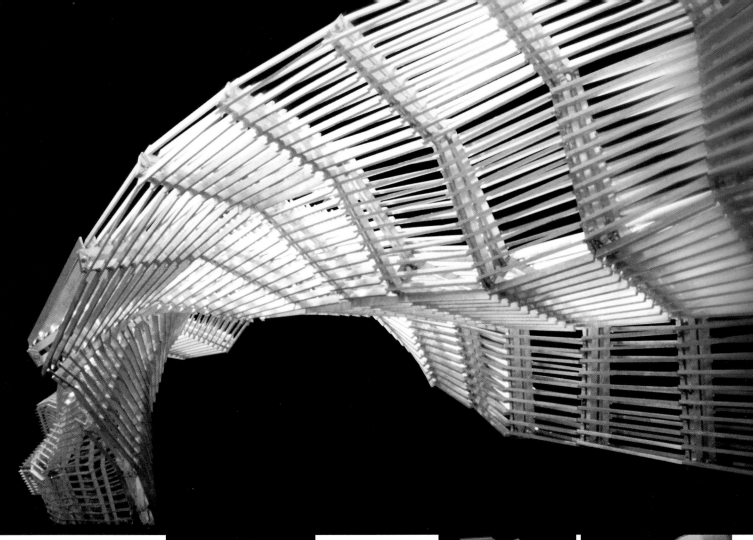

Misericord to a
Grotesque Reification[1]

The widespread adoption of innovative animation techniques is not in itself remarkable. For Mark Goulthorpe of dECOI, the wider significance of the 'cognitive desire to animate' lies in its infiltration of the cultural psyche. With the shift from what he defines as the 'autoplastic' to the 'alloplastic', he looks to a shift from determined creative relationships to one in which reciprocity comes to the fore. Favouring reification (the transformation of the abstract into the concrete) over the grotesque figurative and pictorial tradition of animation, he looks beyond the problems of representation to a future of iconoclastic infinity, which leaves even the notion of multiple images behind.

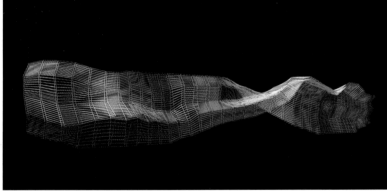

ETHER/I, Geneva, 1995
Ether/I was developed for the 50th anniversary of the United Nations in Geneva, where we traced sequences of Quintett, a ballet by William Forsythe, in which five bodies describe an endlessly unconsummated series of couplings, described by him as a 'representation of loss'. We captured not the positive trace of the disappearing dance, but the difference between attempts at a repeated sequence, the invisible yet vital aspect of a live performance, seeking the recessive sense that the ballet engenders. In celebration of a body that comes into existence only at the moment of suspension or absence, this fissure of failure becomes animate at many other levels than a simple frozen movement. The process, in fact, was one of blatant technical imprecision.

Opposite top
Final form, fabricated from 4,000 bars of aluminium, poised as a virtual object.

Opposite bottom left
A trace of disappearance: the difference between attempts at a repeated sequence of the dance, by the Frankfurt Ballet.

Opposite bottom centre and right
The final sampling of movement extraction.

Above top
The tessellated aluminium surface gives a phantomatic and highly variable optikinetic to the animate form.

Above middle
Final form, dissolving into moiré patterning with the passage of the sun, alternating between ephemerality and agressivity.

Above bottom
The trace form 'back-focused' into definition: two layers of tessellated aluminium.

Design team: Mark Goulthorpe, Zainie Zainul, Wilf Sinclair, Rachel Doherty, Matthieu le Savre.
Computer modelling: Michel Saup, Frankfurt. Dancers: Joni and Jacopo, The Frankfurt Ballet.
Engineering: David Glover of Group IV Ove Arup & Partners, London. Fabrication: Optikinetics, Luton.

... what game is it these artists were playing? – it is the game of 'animation'. Like all games it hovers between believing and pretending. Need I again invoke the 'hobby horse' which is playfully turned into a 'pretend' horse by transforming the end of a stick into a head? Behind the game, I contended, is the desire to ride a horse ... Ernst Gombrich[2]

We would do well to insist that movement is implicit and not explicit in animation, if only to remind ourselves that even with the apparent radicalism of Walt Disney movement is an illusion. Even as the technical means become available to flirt with dynamic possibilities of form, such as those deployed in our Aegis Hyposurface,[3] we should continually reflect on the latent or virtual dynamism that seems to be the essential kernel of animation. Rodin, we remember, decried Muybridge in his claim to having captured movement in his freeze-frame sequencing, accusing him that he had instead frozen it, pinned it like a dead moth.[4] We might then ponder the animate frenzy of Rodin's bronzes, wrought by hand, which seem much more powerfully to be 'actualizing the virtual',[5] capturing the cinematic moment, than the literal capture of movement effected by a new technology. Perhaps one might consider this as the difference between the creation of an image of technological potential and the capture of a technic effect, the pursuit of a displaced cognitive desire. For technological change becomes interesting only insofar as it infiltrates cultural psychology and suggests new patterns of behaviour and expectation. In the story of the monkey with the stick wiggling ants from an ant hill, technology does not reside in the inanimate prosthesis, but first in its proprioceptive fusion with the body, and then in the intersection of a heightened technical potential with the desire for ants that it propagates.[6] The monkey becomes, in fact, ant-mad!

Perhaps it is not stating the obvious to suggest that animation animates(!), produces an effect in us, as a psychological rather than a simply physical manifestation. This demands that we consider it in both a productive and receptive sense, the bodies of the monkey-becoming-man yearning for, and struggling with, the products of a potential and uncertain formal register. In this sense animation may be contrasted with stylisation as noted by Ernst Gombrich in his insightful study in the psychology of decorative art, *The Sense of Order*:

[Stylisation] imposes order and approximates the living form to geometric shapes, [animation] imbues the shapes with life and therefore with movement and expression. That the principle of animation rules unchecked in the world of the grotesque needs no demonstration. The potentially magic function of animation may contribute to our understanding of these forms. For animation not only uses monsters, it generates them ...[7]

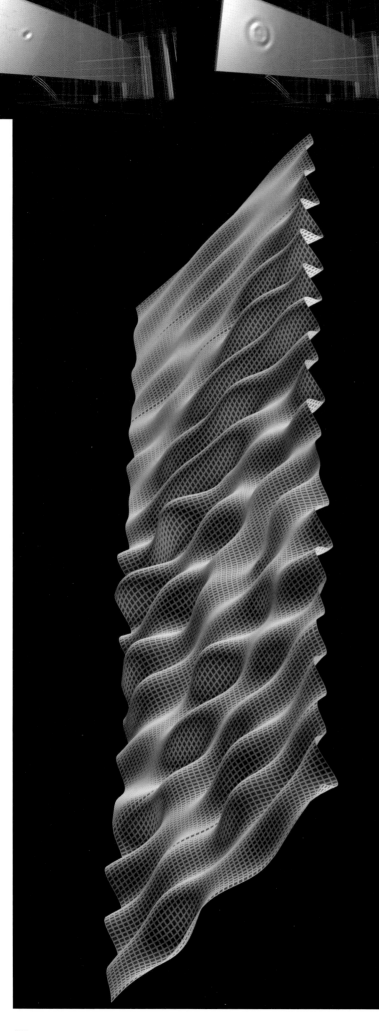

AEGIS Hyposurface, Birmingham, 1999
The Aegis Hyposurface is a kinetic-art project in which a faceted metallic surface is driven by 1,000 actuators controlled by a powerful computational device. This permits the surface to be dynamically reconfigured real-time, activated by a series of electronic sensors (movement, sound, light, etc) which deploy an endlessly variable series of mathematical terrains. But despite its actual dynamic potential, it will be the psychological effect of such endlessly disappearing decora(c)tion, drifting between abstract reification and figurative animation, that will be most suggestive as to the potential trauma offered by such technological latency.

Left
Aegis Hyposurface.

Top
Aegis Hyposurface.

Design team: Mark Goulthorpe, Mark Burry, Oliver Dering, Arnaud Descombes. Technical design: Professor Mark Burry of Deakin University, Australia, with Grant Dunlop. Programming: Peter Wood, University of Wellington, New Zealand. System engineering/design: Chris Glasow of Andromeda Telematics, London. Mathematical studies: Dr Alex Scott and Professor Keith Ball of University College London. Engineering: David Glover of Group IV Ove Arup & Partners, London. Facade consultant: Sean Billings of Billings Design Associates. Rubber research.

Hystera Protera, Modus Operandi Graphics, 1996 (opposite)
This project was developed as an experiment in form-finding, generating a series of three-dimensional glyphs by processes of mapping and morphing. Series and series of analphabets were derived from a single operational process, which gave layer upon layer of serial trace forms along whose axes enigmatic grotesques (or grottes) unfurled as trappings (capture and decoration) of movement – what we termed hyster(a)ics! Curiously caught between two-dimensional and three-dimensional reading, between text and form, such abstract calligraphs also oscillate between figurative and nonfigurative readings. One notes that the very rationality of such a process (every trace form derives from a common origin) suggests the possibility of the drollery becoming structural, of the animate marginal flourish occupying the central ground ...

Opposite left
Hystera Protera: genera(c)tion of serial analphabets by processes of three-dimensional mapping and morphing.

Opposite right, middle
Hystera Protera: three-dimensional mappings as a form of 'primary' (genera(c)tive) memory.

Opposite right, top
Hystera Protera: serial combinations of trace forms give dynamic spatial possibility.

Opposite right, bottom
Hystera Protera: serial combinations of trace forms give dynamic spatial possibility.

Design team: Mark Goulthorpe, Arnaud Descombes.

The condition of the animate is then two-faced, a grotesque product of a monstrous birth-process.[8] Our interest in animation lies in the 'dragon force'[9] required to release new forms to cultural imagination, the muscular birthing of an infant electronic sense that has liquefied the notion of time as being simply a sequence of frozen moments. The temporal sense of computer genera(c)tion seems to suggest a much more fluid and malleable sense of animate potential, where form occurs as the condensation of a 'genetically' embedded variability, form held as a parametrically unstable elastic potential, a sort of conceptual trembling. The form is latent, carries within it many other possibilities.

It therefore seems no longer sufficient to impart a 'field of force'[10] by way of a gravitational or symbolic direction – the grotesques and drolleries of Albrecht Dürer's prayer book for the Emperor Maximillian, or likewise the enigmatic scribbles of Paul Klee, becoming animate at the instant such 'Traumwerk'[11] pulls in a certain direction. Doubtless one must work harder to devise creative parameters which might yield a more complex vectorial potential ...

In this we might follow Gombrich in his separation of animation from reification, reserving for animation figurative (animal/vegetable) directionality where eyes, mouths, tails or gravity impart an animate force to otherwise abstract forms. Reification then refers to the fascination with the sense of movement itself, in nonfigurative inflections, which perhaps serves better in describing current psychologies with their preference for still-abstract form.

At the Morphe[12] conference Greg Lynn alluded to a 'geological' potential that might be trapped in form as the result of using animation software, which he illustrated with reference to an installation that seemed to offer both cognitive and literal disorientation: 'Where's the centre?' uttered in the course of an impelled peripheral movement. The suggestion is compelling for its promise that the adoption of a new technical apparatus, which apparently folds time into the creative process in a literal sense, might spontaneously yield 'animate' form which activates both mental and physical capacity. Doubtless such bold claims are haunted by the spectre of Rodin, and even by Gombrich who asserts that, 'vital to our understanding of these effects is that the uncertainty of response carries over from the perceptual to the emotional sphere ... A fresh effect depended on changes being

Notes
1. Misericords are the small shelf-like seats allowed to monks in the Middle Ages as support during long periods of prayer. In the northern tradition these were frequently embellished by the carpenters with discreet yet frivolous carvings as a physical form of marginal drollery that would serve to refresh and stimulate during worship. See Ernst Gombrich, 'The Edge of Chaos' in The Sense of Order, Phaidon Press, London, 1984 edition, pp 251–284.
Throughout this essay I refer to the grotesque as deriving from the description of the infamous and overdecorated cellars of Rome (the term grotesque derives from grottes, or cave) in which were portrayed all manner of dream-like zoomorphic creatures. I follow Ernst Gombrich's suggestion that the grotesque differs from the drollery in its generally asymmetric form, and in its overt antagonism to accepted aesthetic norms. Reification is distinguished from animation by Gombrich, as noted in the body of the text, a useful but perhaps finally unstable pair of terms.
2. Ibid, p 273.
3. The Aegis Hyposurface project is covered in Mark Goulthorpe, 'dECOi Aegis Hyposurface: Autoplastic to Alloplastic' in Hypersurface Architecture II, Architectural Design, vol 69, no 9–10, Sept/Oct 1999, pp 60–65.
4. Rodin's critique is developed in his famous conversations with Paul Gsell in l'Art: Entretiens reunis par Paul Gsell, 1911.
5. Gilles Deleuze and Felix Guattari's cultural axiom which they contrast to the 'realization of the possible'. To actualise a new potential

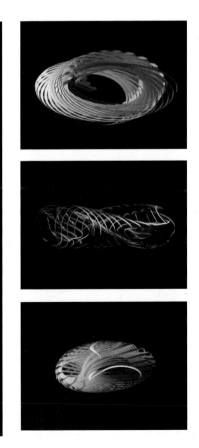

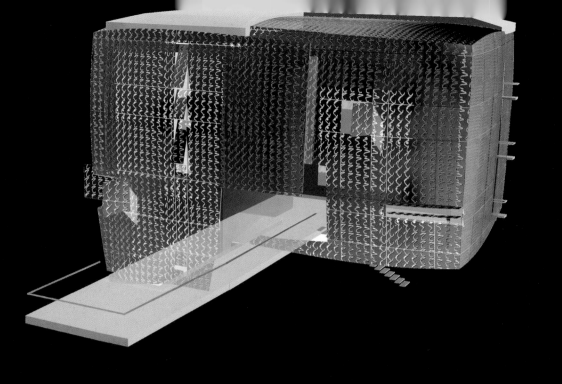

Pallas House, Bukit Tunku, Malaysia, 1997

The Pallas House, designed with Objectile, looked to trapping such hyster(a)ics in material form, where a complex-curved surface was to be numeric-command machined with a transformative series of perforations – a filter to the tropical climate. The idea was to also open the holes wider to the east, and close them smaller to the west, to allow a sort of frozen climatic responsiveness. What began as a quite abstract exercise in pattern-making, which looked merely to generate an intense surface tactility, ended with the generation of several different types of motif which opened an entirely cultural discussion; the (Chinese) client was highly attuned to the figurative implication of such calligraphy. Indeed, on reflection, such uni-décor is characteristic of Chinese patterning, where the surfaces are animated with countless intertwined dragons. As a birthing of now-digital dragons, the surface seems to oscillate between abstract and figurative readings, between a sense of reification and animation, hypnosis and hallucination ...

Above top
Pallas House: a dynamic and serially
transformative uni-décor.

Bottom
Interior shot
Pallas House: decora(c)tive surfaces
creating a luminous arabesque.

Design team: Mark Goulthorpe, Matthieu le Savre, Karine Chartier, Nadir Tazdait, Arnaud Descombes, with Objectile (Bernard Cache, Patrick Beaucé). Engineers: David Glover, Sean Billings and Andy Sedgewick of Group IV Ove Arup & Partners, London.

is to attain a virtual potential which the simple utilisation of a new technique will fall short of. See Gilles Deleuze and Felix Guattari, *1000 Plateaus: Schizophrenia and Capitalism*, University of Minnesota Press Minneapolis, 1980.

6. The monkey-stick story, which concerns the psychological infusion of any technology into cultural desire is recounted in my letter in *AnyMore*, MIT Press, 2000, pp 206-07. The image of technology', which we are apt to dwell upon (the stick, ruined ant hills and a fat monkey) seem as nothing compared to what I term the 'technic-effect' which is the desire for ants that it propagates (cf Rodin/Muybridge, above).

7. Ernest Gombrich, ibid, pp 261-62.

8. These terms are used by Gombrich in trying to account for the psychology of grotesques and drolleries and the animate sense they impart.

9. 'Dragon force' is a term used by the Swedish Sinologist Karlgren to describe the numinous power of the elaborate surfaces of ancient Chinese vessels in which the accumulation of many hundreds of motifs (dragons) engender a quite vertiginous effect. See Gombrich, ibid, pp 262.

10. 'Field of force' is a term used by Gombrich to describe the way in which several motifs may work together to give an impression of movement. See Gombrich, 'Some Musical Analogies' in *The Sense of Order*, p 297.

11. Traumwerk (dreamwork) is a term used by Albrecht Dürer in describing his grotesques and drolleries: 'whoever wants to do dreamwork must mix all things together.' See Gombrich, ibid, p 251.

12. The Oceanic Architecture conference *Morphe* took place at Deakin University in Australia in the summer of 1997. Its specific focus (and hence its name) was on the generation of form within the context of technical (electronic) change.

13. Gombrich, ibid.

14. See Bernard Cache, 'Digital Dragons', *Hyx*, Paris, 1999.

15. See Mark Goulthorpe, 'The Active Inert: Notes on Technic Praxis', *AA Files*, 37; for an extended discussion of the different approaches of Greg Lynn/Form and dECOi to actualising the virtual potential of new technology.

16. A zoomorphic juncture is the fanciful combination of animal and human forms which can be observed as a widespread cultural phenomenon in quite disparate

rung on the psychological reactions to be engaged.'[13] It is the psychological effects engendered by an electronic economy that here seem to offer more potential than the image of frozen mathematics, 'digital dragons'[14] destined to remain inanimate in the absence of a cogent cultural traumwerk.[15]

Where zoomorphic junctures[16] might have been sufficient to destabilise the medieval imagination, the essentially morphic nature of electronic operations renders such techniques effete, digital dragons requiring not simply a problematised representative capacity, but a suspension of all possibility of representative stasis. This conjures up an image of a 'uni-décor'[17] no longer of iconographic multiplicity (such as the interlaced dragon surfaces of ancient China), but of iconoclastic infinity; what we might call an icon-elasticity, the open-ended emergence of textural force. Such is the 'accumulation'[18] of the Aegis Hyposurface, where patterns are deployed as endlessly unstable derivatives, oscillating between hypnotic and hallucinogenic modes, the limits of optic sense, even fading between figurative and abstract patterning. Here the question of the emergence and dissipation of pattern, ornament and writing is floated, rippling back and forth across temporalising modes of thought. An effect of

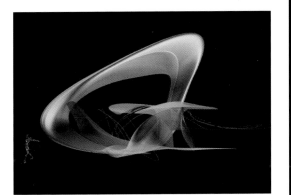

This page
Paramorph: elevation.

Design team: Mark Goulthorpe, Gabriele Evangelisti, Gaspard Giroud, Felix Robbins. Parametric design: Professor Mark Burry of Deakin University, Australia, with Greg More, Grant Dunlop, Andrew Maher. Mathematical studies: Dr Alex Scott, University College London. Engineers: David Glover of Group IV Ove Arup & Partners, London. Model: Grant Dunlop, Deakin University.

PARAMORPH (Gateway to the South Bank), London, 1999
The Paramorph project emerged from studies of the dynamic and ephemeral aspects of the site (movement, sound, etc) to create a gateway of animate reciprocity. At least a dozen formal and social studies are implicated in its sheathing form, which was to serve as a site for the deployment of sound sculpture, triggered by the activity of passers-by. No longer simply a demarcation of cultural threshold, the project is a zone in depth, a giant aural canal attuned to the patterns and rhythms of people in movement. It comes into being as a cultural gateway only in the endless redeployment of everyday patterns of urban activity, and through the very ambiguity of its site-sampled form.

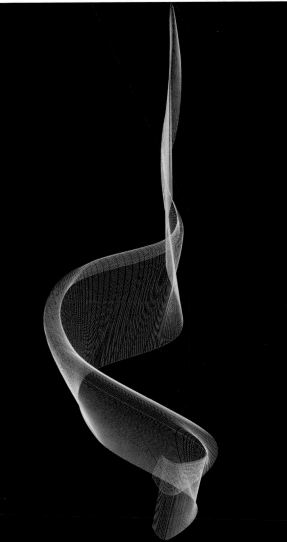

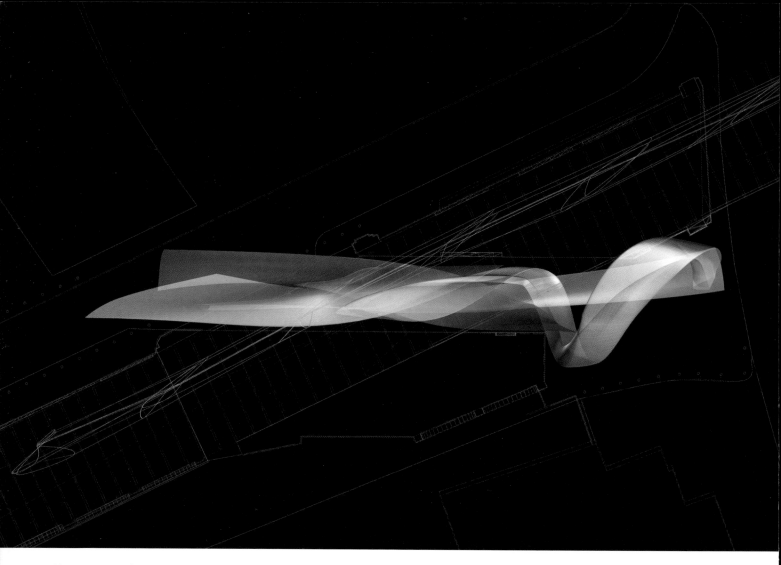

Above
Paramorph: site plan.

Right
Paramorph: section.

Opposite
Paramorph: section through
passage and viaduct.

cultures. See Gombrich, ibid, 'The Edge of Chaos', pp 261–62.

17. 'Uni-décor' is a term used by Kalgren to describe the effect of surfaces in which no part was left undecorated, culminating, for instance, in the great 'dragon force' of certain vessels and objects. See Gombrich, ibid, 'The Edge of Chaos', pp 261–62.

18. Accumulation refers to the numinous power of such supersaturate decorative surfaces, which are announced, albeit crudely, in the potential of the Aegis Hyposurface.

19. Animatism is an awe-struck recognition of the forces of life, an almost religious response to the strange and the terrible. Longman's English Larousse.

20. Picnolepsy is a condition in which there is a momentary blackout of experience which frequently leads to the picnoleptic overinventing to account for the absence of memory. In this sense it provokes a generative, or primary, memory. A good account is given in Paul Virilio, The Vision Machine, publisher (location), date, page/s.

21. See Jay Frankel, 'Ferenczi's Trauma Theory' in The American Journal of Psychoanalysis, vol 58, 1998, page/s; and my extended discussion, 'dECOI Aegis Hyposurface: Autoplastic to Alloplastic'.

animatism[19] at a moment of mnemonic exposure, a picnoleptic[20] absenting that nonetheless triggers imagination.

Doubtless there will always be a tension between the figurative and nonfigurative aspects of any animate form or surface, and perhaps this is what gives it such mental impulsion. The Pallas House, where we mapped lines onto rotating solids as a means of generating a heave or flutter to the surface by the serially transformative perforations of the curved skin, might be seen as stimulating a sense of reification. But in fact the client was Chinese, and we worked hard to appease his particular cultural sensibility in the writhing motifs. Likewise the Paramorph project, derived by a series of quite abstract studies of the dynamic aspects of the site (sound and movement), and defined precisely by a series of quite abstract (geometric) parametric models, nonetheless gapes at the 'head' and accelerates at the 'tail', terms which we used throughout the project as a means of orientation and to give a sense of implied movement.

What this suggests is a representative switching between different readings, which demands articulating in terms of its effect, or the effect of the effect, whereby the motivated glyphs of the Hystera Protera project, for instance, alternate between spatial and graphic tracery. Such significant altercation, and the animate character that it captures, seems to suggest an implicit shift in cultural mode, marking the passage to species of instability and impulsion, born in the move from an autoplastic to an alloplastic tendency. These are Sandor Ferenczi's psychological terms,[21] where 'autoplastic' presumes a determinate relationship between environment and creative/receptive 'self', whilst 'alloplastic' denotes a malleable relationship suggestive of a mode of (unassimilable) cultural reciprocity.

A misericord is the small shelf provided in the Middle Ages to offer some respite to monks at prayer. Traditionally the carpenters were given freedom to carve the invisible misericords as they pleased, and they offered a humorous and variable counterpoint to the otherwise prescribed nature of the liturgy. They were used, in other words, to animate the monks both mentally and physically, the tactile shapes teasing at the contemplative imagination. Frequently such carvings were grotesques or drolleries, bizarre flights of creative impulse that went far beyond representative expectation. Here we invoke the misericord by way of offering a prod in the rear of a system of faith in frozen mathematics that seems to be a substitute for an engagement with the psychologies of perception released in the interstices of technological change. If behind the impulse of the hobby horse lies the desire to ride horses, then the current fascination with animate form must also be articulated in terms of its desire ... △

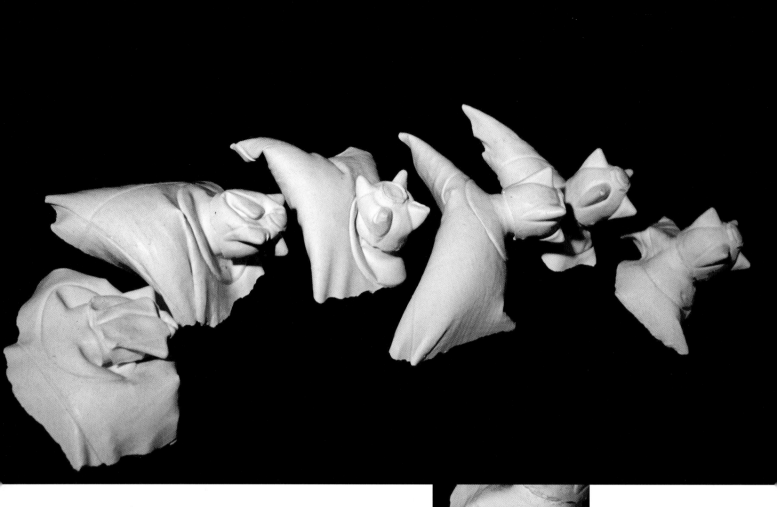

The Will to
Animation

As the current architectural horizon 'squirms with gesticulations',
Pia Ednie-Brown explores the political potential within capacities
for active transformation. Controversially, she argues that the
critical traditions of the American schools have tended to be
dislocated from this potential through an overt privileging of
intellectual structures. Through her own sculptural research and
the designs of Tom Kovac and Jessica Lynch, she investigates a
politics ingrained within manners of working that entail actively
diverse, supple synthesis: a politics of 'the will to animation'.

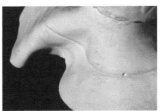

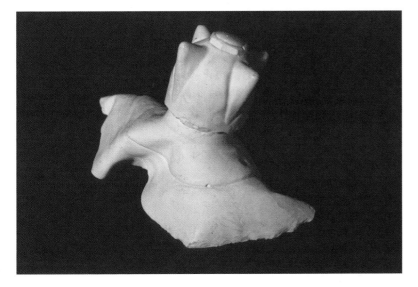

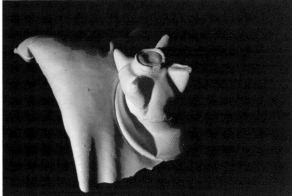

The recent rise of interest in animation within architecture operates in conjunction with a field of contemporary work in which we find phenomena such as buildings involving explicit movement, generative processes involving animation software and the proprioceptive sways of curvilinearity.[1] The horizon squirms with overt gesticulations. Here, architecture becomes an animated diagrammatics madly throwing its arms about in a sign language of qualitative affect: a dancing to the beat of the animate. That which I see as the substance within this architectural turn is referred to here as 'the will to animation': a concept twisted out of Nietzsche's 'Will to Power'. This substance is built up through a capacity for supple transformations that are poignantly politic and of particular relevance to the very animated forms of power that are moulding contemporary political landscapes.

I explore this here through three specific works, each of which has been produced in association with the School of Architecture and Design at RMIT University, Melbourne. These are the work of Tom Kovac, a final year thesis project by student Jessica Lynch and an exploratory project from my own research. These have been bought together for the ways in which they engage very different techniques of animation and the divergent paths through

which they tend toward the production of the animate. Each brings forward issues regarding how things are made, the complexities through which they emerge and the capacity of a process to accept and synthesise a diversity of contingencies. These issues are of key significance to the will to animation; where the 'unity' of this 'will' only exists through a dynamic synthesis of many.

The first example is a series of casts that emerged through my experiments with latex and plaster. Each one of the series is the product of a deformation of the same mould. They were made through pouring liquid plaster into the latex mould of a shower tap. The act of making involved a kind of puppeteering act in which the elastic moulds were suspended with string, positioned with wire and held down with tape under chairs, in boxes, off coat hangers – whatever was at hand. Pouring in the plaster was always a somewhat precarious operation and could never be completely controlled. The latex stretched and deformed with the weight of the fluid plaster, particularly as the makeshift supports fell away or shifted. The resulting casts arose from the coalescing involutions of a myriad of variable relations all struck into an accord: form extracted from dynamic interactions, falling into one another in a collaborative agreement with a responsively overarching skin. This skin becomes a dominant force of *willingness:* a will to formal tendency, but also a willingness to remain sensitive to the materials and conditions with which it engages. The overarching

This spread
'The Turn On', plaster casts,
Pia Ednie-Brown.

definition of the skin held the capacity to deform without falling apart and to transform without entirely losing recognition. This process diagrams the principle of the will to animation.

What becomes important is not simply the emergent form but also an emergent 'texture', where texture is defined as a *tendency of variation*; a flexible refrain; a variable consistency. This shift from form to texture involves the transformation of 'materiality', from a reduction to the forms and qualities of visible material to a more extensive and inclusive *materiality of affect*,[2] wherein the animate (virtuality) becomes palpable.

The 'character-like' qualities of the casts act through a sense that every modulation operates in accord with every other; all are swept into a spring of suspended animation. There is a lightness or levity that emerges through this intertwinement or fall of conditions and signs into one another. One of the most significant moves made in the shift from the moulded metal shower-tap to the plaster casts is the escape from the straight jacket of the rigid mould. The moulds which shape the taps in our bathrooms are not endowed with a flexibility that allows

register. The viscerality of duration or the force of expression is both violently and subtly suppressed. Alternatively, where the primary register of variable relations (the mould), or that which holds a primary power to affect, *retains the power to be affected* it acts to affirm rather than suppress the virtuality that stirs within it in the encounters in the act of emergence. *'To affirm is not to take responsibility for, to take on the burden of what is, but to release, to set free what lives.* To affirm is to unburden: not to load life with the weight of higher values, but to create new values which are those of life, which make life light and active.'[4] It is escaping from lofty weights through the capacity 'to laugh, to play and to dance.'[5]

The politics of the rigid mould is to render that which falls under its arch of influence as submissive and servile. Deviation and deformation become aberrant, invalid, illegal. The politics of the flexible mould is one of an affirmation of the force of expression in its multiplicity.

The politics of these casts provided a way through which to understand the practice of Tom Kovac. Making sense of his work is a manifold operation mainly because it is so many: so many moments folded into the one, so many trajectories synthesised within the surface, so many sounds when nothing seems to be said. The work does not emerge through stating a position or staking out its place within a cognitive territory or processual strategy through which it will move. Rather, it shifts through different territories with supple modulations, transforming in relation to the forces it encounters while holding together through the flexible integrity of its tendencies of variation. The attention Kovac's architecture has sustained is linked with its capacity to move with the flows of the current; to dance around the props of the proper.

The supple synthesis at work in Kovac's practice is not contained in the expressed physical actualisations, but is nonetheless inseparable from them. The sense that a singular quality of force is gathered through the overtly smooth interrelation of elements is very powerful – both within each project and, variably, across the body of work. Windows stretch away, as much as possible, from being distinct frames, always slipping into surfaces which encounter minimal interruption; floors become part of an enveloping surface so that the ground swirls up over one's head; colour is uncompromisingly focused (all white, all red – any additional elements: grey or black); detailing operates to minimise discontinuities; furniture is peeled back into singular gestures so that it can enter into, rather than disrupt, the flow through which the architecture is swept. Everything is, as much as possible, moved into a differential continuity of variation.

This is what we can directly witness in an encounter with his work, but there is an infinitely more expansive

The overarching definition of the skin held the capacity to deform without falling apart and to transform without entirely losing recognition. This process diagrams the principle of the will to animation.

them to be affected by the material they set into shape (they have to remain unaffected in order to ensure that each one of a series of casts are identically formed).

The processual assembly line through which standardised elements are formed has a very definite consistency of action, but this process strives to remain consistently *the same* rather than *differentially* consistent. Standardised elements are no more or less expressive of the consistency of their formation than more flexible ones. What becomes most important is the capacity for the *dominant force* (the mould) to be affected by that with which it engages: *'In order for the will to power to be able to manifest itself it needs to perceive the things it sees and feel the approach of what is assimilable to it.'*[3] Standardised formations speak most emphatically of a distant regime, bearing a heavy shadow of the rigidity for which they act as a

Above
Ikon Tower, Tom Kovac. Digital
Imaging, Jonathon Duckworth

Opposite
Glow Bar, Tom Kovac,
Melbourne, Australia.
Photography John Gollings

terrain of forces that can never be seen and can only be sensed (the determined passion, site conditions, economics and sponsorship deals, conversations, the turbulence of travel ...). All is choreographed in gyrating concert and coalesced through the force of a fiercely focused, flexible expression: into the force of a fiercely focused 'differential mutual emergence'.[6] A diagram of the process of becoming.[7]

These gestural sweeps operate with such flexible determination (rather than rigid determinism) that operations of materiality make an emphatic move through the assemblage of individual materials into a materiality of affect.[8] The animate made palpable. A pulse of sensation passes through the architectural body, translating and synthesising stimuli in choreographically transforming it into a wave of vibrations, rhythms, contractions and expansions;

'...the capacity for being affected is not necessarily a passivity but an *affectivity*, a sensibility, a sensation.'[9]

The coincidence of Kovac's work and the deformed tap-casts lies in the common departure from rigid moulds of instrumentality. This can be counterpoised with the critical tradition of the American schools, which has operated through a *privileging* of intellectual structures that, in order to be critical, survey the process of design from a distance. When the dominant force, or the primary limits of process, form through a foregrounding of intellectual structures the processual mould is more or less characterised by rigidity, representational distance and formalised relationships. This approach is ingrained in the work of Peter Eisenman, where he insists on distance in order to avoid the danger of impotence through absorption into dominant flows of power. As he writes in his recent book, *Diagram Diaries*:

One of the pitfalls of modern architecture was that it attempted to express the zeitgeist in its being rather than displacing it. Ultimately, modern architecture was absorbed by global capital, precisely because the ideology of modernism became normal and generic rather than critical ... The possibility of such a global capital today is a manifestation of the failure of modernism to transgress and displace its own space. In its attempt to manifest that zeitgeist, modern architecture lost the possibility for displacement and presentness ...[10]

If it can be said, as I did above, that Kovac's work has the capacity to 'move with the flows of the current' then, given the terms that Eisenman lays out, this might cast it down the pit into which modernist architecture fell through its expression of the zeitgeist. But Kovac's is not an expression *of* the zietgeist, it is an emergence that casts its skin *through* a supple interaction *with* the zeitgeist, or the pulse of the moment. Where Eisenman locates the two possibilities of critical displacement or expressive immersion, Kovac operates within a third.

Any historical specificity offers its own forms of danger. We are always negotiating some assemblage of forces which act as dominant regimes and threaten various kinds of violence; some kind of relinquishing of potential. In Gilles Deleuze's paper, *Postscript on Control Societies*, he outlines the shift from disciplinary societies to 'societies of control'; to the conditions and logics which contemporaneity seems to offer. He outlines this as a shift of logic: from a disciplinary logic defined by rigid confinements to one of 'control' defined through modulations. The shift can be tracked across the path from the shower tap to the plaster-cast production, from rigid moulds to flexible ones: 'Confinements are moulds, different mouldings, while controls are a modulation, like a self-transmuting moulding continually changing from one moment to the next, or like a sieve whose mesh varies from one point to another.'[11] This implies a differently constituted set of dangers, where 'a man is no longer a man confined but a man in debt.'[12] But, as he wrote, 'It's not a question of worrying or of hoping for the best, but of finding new weapons.'[13]

Notes
1. For example, such phenomena can be found operating within the investigative concerns of practices such as those of dECOi, NOX, Mark Burry, Tom Kovac, Greg Lynn and Asymptote.
2. For a more detailed exploration of this concept of the 'materiality of affect' see: Pia Ednie-Brown, 'Falling into the Surface', Stephen Perrella (ed), *Hypersurface Architecture* II, *Architectural Design*, vol 69, no 9–10, Sept/Oct 1999, profile 141, pp 8–11.
3. Nietzsche, quoted by Gilles Deleuze, *Nietzche and Philosophy*, Hugh Tomlinson (trans), Athlone Press

Weapons are not *things* but modes of action. Maintaining ideas of resistance is no longer tenable: the opponent moves too fast and changes shape too often. As forms of power become more animated, negotiating them requires the capacity to transform with nimble acumen; to play when the rules need to be manipulated, to dance around the props of the proper, to laugh when the world becomes heavy. To know how to do what lofty regimes cannot subsume: to laugh, to play and to dance.[14] It becomes an issue of gathering enough force and power of expression within the transformations

something else, a freeing of the work from an ideological necessity?[15]

The fate of this ideological substructure lies in the fate of the diagram, which:

... has come full circle from the strategies of reading to the tactics of visceral experience. At the same time, the diagram seems to disappear from the built work ... it becomes more or less a virtual entity, rather than being made explicit in the projects. This is because the diagram becomes more of an engine in the projects rather than something which transforms itself into a physical reality.[16]

As the diagram disappears both into and out of the

of the moment to remain at the surface with depth; to not be subsumed by the current or spread too thin, to not be carried along without any power to affect.

Peter Eisenman's book proclaims great faith in the importance of being critical, but traces out a curve through which the diagram as an instrument of a critical architecture has been forced, more or less against its will, to succumb to something else. *Diagram Diaries* moves sequentially through over 30 years of work mapping out the transformations that have occurred through his investigations which, more than anything else, interrogate the possibilities for intensified criticality in architecture. This critical activity, mapped out and produced through diagrams, is understood as an ideological operation. Towards the end of this text, he writes:

I no longer feel compelled to insist upon an ideological sub-structure in my own work. If one looks back on the work, historically, thirty years from now, will it be said that this loss of ideology was a late period, a playing out of an endgame? Or will it be said that this publication marks a new opening to

projects, this third politics would seem to be the 'opening to something else'.

This emergence suggests a manner of working that slips between, and extends beyond, Eisenman's dichotomy of options. We can find this in Kovac's politics of supple, consistently variational skins: skins which are at once sensitive and brutal; constructively politic; playing with the rules. Transformationally determined. Dangerous and vital in their fabricated realities. Within this Nietzchean playfulness 'laughter flutters from him like a motely cloud.'[17] An imminence of a will to animation. *A diagram of the process of becoming.*[18]

Actual form is immanence as it has folded out of itself.[19]

Within these politics is a concurrent shift related to identity, which is no longer fixed but thoroughly animated. While this is implicit in Kovac's practice, it becomes explicit in the final-year thesis project of Jessica Lynch who worked with the animation of identity as integral to a political architectural act.

Her project sprang out of a competition brief for a public space with ancillary exhibition areas in the parliamentary zone of Canberra. This space was called for in order to mark and celebrate the centenary moment of Australia's federation of states into a political

Above
'Inverted Landscape', final-year thesis project at RMIT, Jessica Lynch. Section through site.

(London), 1983, p 63.
4. Ibid, p 185.
5. As Deleuze writes: 'There are things that the higher man does not know how to do: to laugh, to play and to dance. To laugh is to affirm life, even the suffering in life. To play is to affirm chance and the necessity of chance. To dance is to affirm becoming and the being of becoming.' *Nietzche and Philosophy*, p 170.
6. 'As Guattari never tired of saying, and this essay has just as tirelessly repeated, it is about expression as differential mutual emergence. Autopoiesis.' Brian Massumi,

unity. Operating with a wry humour and a finely tuned attention to delicate absurdities, Jessica set out to transform weighty forms of identity through a series of transformational inversions.

Each state of Australia has an emblematic flower. These became delightfully appropriate pickings which she set out to rearrange, deformationally. From a series of old etchings of these flowers, she modelled them in 3D with AutoCAD where the pastel meshes strangely approximated the fine line-work of hand-drawn etchings. She initially arranged them into a sequential, animated mutation of one flower

'Involuntary Afterward', *Deleuze, Guattari and the Philosophy of Expression*, Brian Massumi (ed), The Canadian Review of Comparative Literature, vol 24, no 3, 1998.
http://www.anu.edu.au/HRC/first and last/works/crclintro.htm
7. 'The form of encounter we extract is not a "form" as we would normally think of one. It is not static. It is a dynamism, composed of a number of interacting vectors. The kind of "unity" it has in no way vitiates that multiplicity – it is precisely an interaction between a multiplicity of terms, an interrelation of relations, an integration of disparate elements. *It is a diagram of the process of becoming*.' Brian Massumi, *A User's Guide to Capitalism and Schizophrenia: Deviations from Deleuze and Guattari*, MIT Press (Cambridge, Mass), 1992, p 14.
8. This might suggest a 'dematerialisation' of texture/substance, which would be misleading. The claim is that materiality is *never* simply located in the static life of materials because it operates more powerfully in the relations between them

into another, so that these icons federated cinematically. In realising the potential within this animated morphology, but wishing to dodge any implied seamless merger of the states, she carried the process into a more complex act where each species was inverted through a rotation of their turning inside out. Here she drew upon the suggestions of E Jouffret[20] that an object turned inside out is rotated through the fourth dimension. What this offers, as Jessica argued via Duchamp's work relating to the multiplicity of identity and the fourth dimension, is an unleashing of the 'potential that we can be everything at once'.[21] The various stages of these inversions became the infinite smorgasbord of formations for the variously programmed pavilions that would be scattered across the new public space. During the process of design development, when these drawings were exposed to others, we would hear sighs, moans and gasps of delight which seemed to echo the transformative action of the flowers moving through the stages of rotational inversion.

These twisted flora fell onto the site in accord with a celestial positioning drawn from the

(and other forces). This
relational 'materiality of affect'
is inseparable from all aspects
of physical actualisation (that
is, it does not replace the
commonly visible, but expands
it).
9. Gilles Deleuze, *Nietzche and
Philosophy*, p 62.
10. Peter Eisenman, *Diagram
Diaries*, Thames and Hudson
(London), 1999, p 43.
11. Gilles Deleuze, 'Postscript
on Control Societies' in
Negotiations, Martin Joughin
(trans), Columbia University
Press (New York), 1995, p 179.
12. Ibid, p 181.
13. Ibid, p 178.

location of the stars above the site at the dawn of Australia's federation. Tall poles pierced each stellar position, becoming primary structural elements for each of the floral pavilions: '… like the pins of a giant butterfly collection. Architectural Entomology.'[22] Across the flat plane of the manicured lawn (so characteristic of Canberra) she laid down an image of a woman published in the *Bulletin* newspaper in 1899 as a caricature of the emerging about-to-be-federated nation standing in wanton shame as Australian soldiers set out to fight battles for the British Empire. This image, which we came

transformed through the lightness of a playfully transformative laughter. In mustering up some sense of 100 years of 'Australiana' the momentum became as much an entropic one as a coagulation. The becoming of a federated body is here not celebrated as a unified prow on the sea of nations. Rather, her scheme literally turns enclosed identities or specified states inside out and casts them into a suspended sea of interconnected, multiplicitous transformation. Moments of singular identity are instituted only in order to feel them fall apart, transform and multiply in accord with the reverberations of a laughter that sensitively unfolds through a will to animation.

The will to animation is not a matter of rushing out to make things move, but a question of the terms through which architecture becomes animate as a technology in itself.

14. See note 5.
15. Peter Eisenman, *Diagram
Diaries*, p 207.
16. Ibid, pp 208–9.
17. Nietzche, *Thus Spoke
Zarathustra*, quoted in *Gilles
Deleuze, Nietzche and
Philosophy*, p 171.
18. See note 7.
19. Brian Massumi,
'Involuntary Afterward', op cit.
20. E Jouffret, *Trait
elementaire de geometrie a
quatre dimensions*, Gauthiers-
Villars (Paris), 1903.
21. Jessica Lynch, final design
thesis statement, November
2000.
22. Ibid.
23. Ibid.

to know as 'Miss Fed' (or misfed), was radically stretched along the primary parliamentary axis so that it would anamorphically reconstitute into the original from a tourist lookout (through viewing binoculars or those touristic coin-operated peepshows of picturesque moments). This 'point of hindsight'[23] is positioned at the viewpoint of the surveyor in Marion Mahony's early illustration of the Canberra master plan, designed by herself and Walter Burley Griffin. While the identification of this image was retained at this one poignantly hingeful moment, it was thoroughly unrecognisable from any other point of view. The black-and-white newspaper etching became an inverted mould, carved as an inverse figure out of the ground, a dug-out sculpted terrain that formed an 8 metre wide, 80 metre long, axial scar across the lawn. This depression of modulated landform became a vast linking chasm between the pavilions which danced about its sides.

Jessica's work is thick with cultural signs and densely packed with layers of narrative significance. She has cleverly managed to choreograph this weighty depth into a synthesis wherein the cultural gravity of the project is

The will to animation is not a matter of rushing out to make things move (even though this may well be involved), but a question of the terms through which architecture becomes animate as a technology in itself. In it, architecture realises its potential as an animated diagram; a diagram of the process of becoming.

At the beginning of this paper I referred to the substance within the architectural turn to animation. The case studies above have been explored for the various ways in which this substance is built up through a supple intertwinement of forces. Each presents a politics which depart from regimes of distant instrumentality, the confinements of standardisation and rigid identities. They cast off such heavy shadows through an animated politics that enables the affirmation of potential and the power to be affected. The turn of architectural attention to the animate is a substantial twist that cannot be reduced to opportunism in the face of new technologies such as advanced animation software. It is a twist impelled by shifts and bends in the fibres of social, political assemblages. But this is not a shift from one posture to another, it is a movement that adheres only to movement: movement that gathers power through the capacity to operate through supple transformation and complex synthesis; through the will to animation. ∆

Opposite
'Inverted Landscape', final
year thesis project at RMIT,
Jessica Lynch. Rotational
inversion of orchid flower
through itself with diagram
of inversion process.

Dendrobium bigibbum, Cooktown orchid

The Design Implications of Mass Customisation

It is not only designers who are excited by the latent potential of animatory and other computerised techniques. As Tim Crayton, a consultant on marketing and design, outlines, the implications of tailoring products more closely to the demands of individual consumers are set to revolutionise production. How far, however, will mass customisation go, and will architects really be prepared to become co-designers?

Computerisation has had a profound impact on all aspects of design: it has changed both its how and its what of design. Not only has it transformed design processes and design economics, it has also transformed the nature of the products that can be created. For example, CAD allows teams of designers and other professionals to collaborate in new ways, to visualise different alternatives and try out different options; to keep options open longer, design different alternatives in parallel and pick up the problems sooner. The design software that designers use has moved from being a tool to being an intelligent environment that can guide and inform the design process. Design software has become smart and the expertise of expert systems forms a network of helpers and/or 'embedded critics'.[1] In short, CAD enables designers to be more creative and effective *qua* designers.

It has also made it possible to communicate design ideas and concepts to others more effectively, whether they be marketers, finance directors, focus groups, planner or clients and other so-called 'silent designers'[2] – other non-designers who determine design outcomes. One of the most important uses of visualisation software is selling, and in the property market VR walkthroughs have, of course, become a marketing tool for large development projects and individual flat sales.

Computerised design may have made designers better at designing and enhanced existing marketing strategies and channels, but advances in CAD, together with changes in production technologies (in particular the integration with CAM) and organisational methods, have the potential to radically change the industrial design processes that have developed over the last century.

The technologies that make designers better designers can be put – with suitable adjustments and refinements – in the hands of non-designers, including consumers and end-users, to allow them to configure, or even co-design, products by interacting directly with highly flexible manufacturing systems. Instead of *designing for consumers*, CAM systems will enable *design by consumers*.[3]

In some ways this is a return to an older preindustrial – or pre-Fordist – paradigm where products were created individually by a process of consultation and collaboration between a designer/producer and a customer. But instead of the relationship being personal and face to face, it can be mediated through information technology.

From Mass Production to Mass Customisation

Since Henry Ford pioneered production-line methods at the beginning of the century, industrialised economies have been based (apart from the survival of usually up market bespoke and craft manufacture and, of course, capital production) on mass production, mass distribution, mass marketing and mass media. However, a combination of advances in information and communication technologies and new manufacturing and design technologies and concepts is making it increasingly possible to 'mass-customise' – to respond rapidly to consumers, with customised products at mass-production prices.

Mass production required standardisation and the concomitant 'logic of aggregation'[4] was dominant in the last century because of the nature of economies of scale not only in manufacturing (resulting from, amongst other things, single-use dedicated machine tools and long set-up times) but throughout the economy. It should be added that one effect was to create large companies[5] and so 'big business'; and indeed one of the functions of mass marketing was not only to create demand but also to raise barriers to entry.[6]

Standardisation can also be seen as part of a management ideology – and maybe even as a political ideology – that was closely related to a lot of design thinking in the 20th century.

Standardisation emerged because in a mass-production system it was, as a matter of objective fact, hard to produce variety. But standardisation can also be seen as part of a management ideology – and maybe even as a political ideology – that was closely related to a lot of design thinking in the 20th century. The well-known management writer Henry Mintzberg emphasises, 'to what extent [standardisation] ... was an act of cognition as well as a reflection of economic and technological forces'.[7]

As well as making it difficult to produce variety, mass production also had implications for the design process. Because products were standardised, producers had to produce products that appealed to mass markets, or at least aggregated groups of consumers, and once these had been created they could not be easily varied. Thus the form of communication between consumers and producers tended to be in one direction at any one time. Hence, once a product was designed, marketing communication tended, certainly after the emergence of TV, to be the one-way broadcast of generalised messages.

Developments such as Rapid Product Development and Concurrent Engineering have clearly changed what can be termed the traditional New Product Development (NPD) process. However, producers still collect customers' opinions in a market research phase, and once a product is designed it is basically not possible to respond, without very expensive 'custom engineering' on a case-by-case basis, to individual demands.

As has been suggested the mass-paradigm was not static. Subsequently Japanese methods of mass production and so-called Lean Production have made it possible to produce high variety. In any case, 'pure standardisation' in the sense of 'any colour so long as it is black' was no longer viable for anyone in the car industry beyond the 1920s. But we now seem to be at another turning point where it is becoming possible not only to produce great variety, but also to produce customisation at the same cost as mass production. Indeed, the vision is of manufacturing systems that will be able to produce whatever you want.

What is 'Mass Customisation'?

The futurist Alvin Toffler first wrote about 'de-standardisation' and 'de-massification'[8] but the term 'mass customisation' was coined (and, it should be stressed, was intended be deliberately paradoxical) by the writer and consultant Stan Davis in his book *Future Perfect*.[9] In fact, the term is somewhat accidental and is really interchangeable with a variety of other labels like 'mass individualisation' and 'individualised mass production', 'machine customisation' or maybe 'flexible production'. But mass customisation stuck and was developed and popularised by Joe Pine.[10] Having started as futurology there is now a large management literature and a range of pioneering companies pursuing 'mass customisation'.

Pretty Good Life

Greg Lynn is the premier architectural pioneer of mass customisation. His Embryologic Houses project (see **ᗳ** Contemporary Processes in Architecture, vol 70, no 3, 2000) created 'a line of one of a kind housing customised for unique people and locations'. His work for PrettyGoodLife is an example of one of the ways he is already starting to realise his ideas.

But clearly mass customisation has very different implications for different products and in different sectors. There are also different methods and strategies to achieve it. In fact, there seem to be at least 20 different overlapping senses of mass customisation. For example, many manufacturers are pursuing greater levels of 'cosmetic customisation' through a greater range of colours, finishes, etc. It may be possible to individualise a product through the surrounding service envelope. Some products can be tailored or customised at the retail outlet or dealer ('post-production customisation'). Other products may adapt to the user, as, for example, the intelligent systems increasingly available in cars, that adapt (transparently) to your style of driving ('adaptive customisation').

But as well as these softer, or 'post-production' forms of customisation it is also possible for the consumer to interact with the design and manufacturing process to alter the design of the core product. For many products this will mean choosing from predefined or configured choices – and perhaps the majority of consumers will be happy with this and won't want to go further. Clearly there seem to be limitations as to how far it will be possible, or desirable, to vary a complex technological product like a car. Although some industry scenarios predict that customers will be able to, in effect, create their own car from different manufacturers' modular subsystems.

But for many products it will be possible to offer much freer or infinite choice. Indeed, the most important distinctions running through all the different senses of mass customisation are at what point the consumer becomes involved (design, fabrication, assembly, or postproduction), to what extent the choice is configured or free and the extent to which the process is 'transparent' or 'collaborative'[11] and forms part of a dialogue between the producer and the customer.

This wide range of meanings of mass customisation is reflected in confusion amongst design professionals. For some designers – especially product designers – mass customisation means a return to the era of the designer – maker and for others – especially design

The showroom concept for PrettyGoodLife.com responds to the need for a mutable brand identity in a variety of contexts throughout the world. Given the same generic design technique, high degrees of variation can be produced for the showrooms which are of various sizes and shapes, in different locales. The interiors are both customised and mass-produced, using advanced computer-controlled manufacturing processes and the control of design variations.

There are two types of construction in the showroom interiors. The first is a liner for the existing spaces. This is designed with gently bulging plaster walls, gradually sloping poured-epoxy floors, aluminium metal trim and frosted-glass luminescent ceilings. Encased within this cleanly defined shell is a second construction that provides for the display of objects of various shapes and sizes. This is like a large piece of furniture as it is built of stained and painted wood walls and cork floors.

The shape of the display vehicle is curvilinear and has a voluptuous undulating interior within which glass shelves nestle. These are manufactured using cnc (computer numerically controlled) cutting robots to achieve their variety and complexity. Rather than a smooth surface, the texture of these panels is designed as a rippling surface that exploits the artefacting of the manufacturing robot. The inner surface of this display vehicle is painted with a subtle Colorshift™ paint that refracts the light and accentuates the visual rippling effect of the surface.

Because the objects displayed in the showroom range in size from tableware to couches, the shelving system has to be extremely flexible. The undulations of the surface provide for both the projection of objects out from the wall and the nesting of smaller objects in niches. A system of stainless-steel display pegs can be inserted across a network of receptacles embedded in the carved wooden blocks of the display wall. The reversible glass shelves have two different curved profiles so that they can be aligned to at least two different positions on the wall. In this way the design achieves a flexible and unique functional scheme within each showroom, as well as a variety of shapes, sizes and configurations in different locations; all of which derive from a single design and construction strategy. Δ

engineers – the only form of true mass customisation is what can be termed design-to-order.

But both these views miss the point: the key to cost-effective customisation is modularisation and configuration. Products are 'decomposed' into modular components or subsystems that can be recombined to more nearly satisfy consumer needs. The other side of the coin is the configuration systems that present the choices to consumers and determine what goes with what.

How Far Will Mass Customisation Go?

Many people will be familiar with some of the examples that show, not only that mass customisation is possible, but also that there seems to be an underlying or latent demand for mass-customised products. One of the best-known examples is, of course, Levi's who offer custom-made jeans. But this relatively simple form of made-to-measure customisation ('dimensional customisation') has already been superseded.

In contrast to Levi's narrow dimensional customisation, the Internet-based manufacturer IC3D™ offers consumers a wide choice of features ranging from thread colour to the type of belt loops, pocket and leg shape. IC3D™ have the following interesting comment on their website.

We applaud companies such as Dell computer and Levi's that provide 'Personal' customization ... but please don't be mistaken and think these companies design their products for you because they don't. Dell offers many configuration choices for your PC but does not design your PC. Levi's does much the same by using a database to search from over 4000 patterns to find the best 'Levi's' pattern for you, but does not design your jeans for you.[12]

By offering a combination of relatively narrow configured choices which are designed-in, as it were, IC3D actually allows consumers to make design decisions which would normally be made by designers. Hence co-design.

Co-design does not have to stop at this kind of configured choice. It is also possible to allow consumers to interact with some of the more subjective elements of the design such as the cut. While the advent of ink-jet print-on-demand technology for fabrics makes it possible for consumers to interact with the design of a fabric to create their own designs, or to at least change the colourways or motifs of fabric designs that have been designed to be co-designed.

A further example worth highlighting is Barbie. Barbie appears to be the archetypal standardised product, indeed it is an archetype. But it is now possible for little girls to configure their own Barbie at the Mattel website[13] by choosing its skin tone, eye and hair colour, hairstyle,

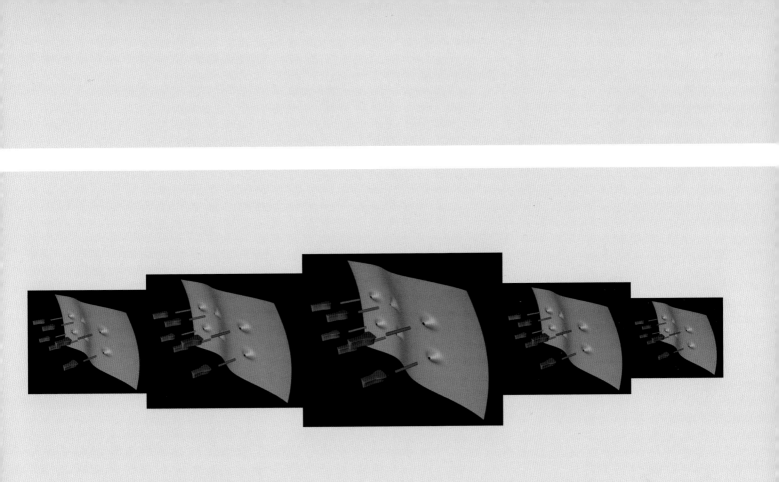

clothes and accessories, and even its name and personal history. Perhaps, as some commentators are suggesting, all products can be customised? This truly would be a paradigm shift from mass production to mass customisation.

Mass Customisation as Co-Design – What are the Issues for the Design Process?

Paradoxically, considering mass customisation's huge significance, there has been little consideration of the implications for design. Or, rather, there is very little about its effect on what can perhaps be termed design with a capital 'D', or visible design, as opposed to the underlying design rules or strategies that make it possible.

At the core of mass customisation is a change in the current relationship between production and consumption. The nature of communication between producer and consumers changes from one-way at any one time to an interactive dialogue. So the marketing function changes from, broadly speaking, selling one-size-fits-all to explaining how products can be customised/ configured and the capabilities of the producer to create products that are more precise solutions to the customers' wants and needs. Consumers will become what Alvin Toffler

Notes
1. G Fisher, K Nakakoji, J Ostwald, G Stahl and T Sumner, 'Embedding Critics in Design Environments' in MT Maybury and W Wahlster (eds), *Intelligent User Interfaces*, Morgan Kaufmann Publishers Inc (San Francisco) 1998, pp 537–59. Reprinted from *The Knowledge Engineering Review Journal*, Special Issue on Expert Critiquing, 8: 4, pp 285–307.
2. P Gorb and A Dumas, 'Silent Design', *Design Studies*, 8: 3 (1987), pp 150–56.
3. M Tseng and X Du, 'Design by Customers for Mass Customization Products', *CIRP Annals*, 47: 1 (1998), pp 103–06.
4. J Lampel and H Mintzberg, 'Customizing Customization',

Paradoxically, considering mass customisation's huge significance, there has been little consideration of the implications for design.

termed, 'prosumers' (Prosumption = Consumption + Production)[14] and co-designers of product-solutions for their individual needs.[15]

Similarly, the task of design will also change. Clearly customisation will, as it were, have to be designed into products. The design task shifts from designing definitive unvariable products to designing product platforms and architectures, and the sets of design rules that define a range of product-solutions. Similarly, the new product design process will also include designing the design tools and interfaces for consumers as co-designers which will configure or determine the kinds of choices consumers will make and perhaps simulate the actual product.

In many ways, this extends the kind of customer involvement that is already seen in concurrent Engineering: it can now be in realtime and on going on an individual basis. Under the heading 'Rethinking Design', the authors of a book on the future of production anticipate some of the ways in which design will change. 'Implicit in creating solution products whose characteristics are jointly defined by producers and customers is a fundamental redefinition of design ... design becomes part of the total production process.'[16]

In this new paradigm the central issue is probably the balance between standardisation, or rather standardised variety, and the relative freedom of choice that consumers are offered – ie. controlled and configured

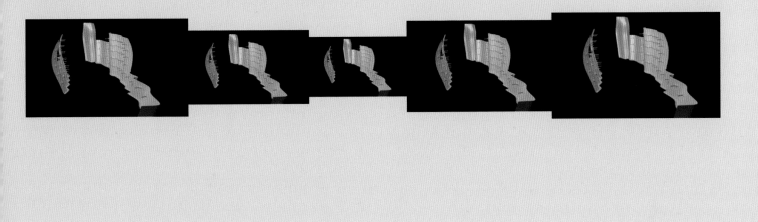

Sloan Management Review, Fall (1996), p 22.

5. AD Chandler, *The Visible Hand: The Managerial Revolution in American Business*, MIT Press (Cambridge, Mass), 1962.

6. Richard S Tedlow, *New and Improved: The Story of Mass Marketing in America*, Heinemann (Oxford), 1990.

7. Lampel and Mintzberg, op cit, p 21.

8. Alvin Toffler, *The Third Wave*, William Morrow & Co (New York), 1980.

9. SM Davis, *Future Perfect*, Addison-Wesley (New York), 1987.

10. JB Pine II, Mass Customisation, *The New Frontier in Business Competition*, HBS Press (Boston) 1993.

11. James H Gilmore and Joseph B Pine II, 'The Four Faces of Mass Customisation', *Harvard Business Review*, January/February (1997), pp 91–101.

12. http://www.ic3d.com/

13. http://www.mybarbie.com/mydesign/

14. Toffler, op cit.

15. LG Goldman, RN Nagel and K Preiss, *Agile Competitors and Virtual Organizations*, Van Nostrand Reinhold (New York), 1996.

16. Goldman, Nagel and Preiss, ibid, p 80.

choice and greater subjective or infinite choice. There are huge questions. There seems to be an underlying demand for customisation, but how much customisation do consumers want? How will it vary from product to product? What will the effects of changes in supply (in one sector) be on demand across the economy? And perhaps above all, what is the best way to interact with consumers as co-designers? And how individual will consumers want to be?

Mass Customisation, Co-Design and Design

The discussion has largely examined the implications of management thinking about mass customisation on product design. What is the implication for architecture? Clearly much has been said about the relation between architecture and industrial design – often to show that modernism and modern architecture is, or was, the inevitable outcome of industrialism. Clearly one, and it should be stressed only one, strand in architectural modernism has been the so-called machine aesthetic. Equally clearly there are strong connections between Fordism and the Scientific Management movement and much architectural thinking in the 20th century.

Perhaps we don't have the same kind of dominant machine ideology any more, but some of the confusion about mass customisation does seem to stem from what are rapidly becoming outmoded ideas about production. The changing nature of machines and machine production, that is smarter, flexible and less mechanistic points to a new kind of machine aesthetic.

Obviously architecture is a complex case since buildings are capital goods. Most building is one-off, although, of course, much of it is designed en masse. Buildings can be unique but are by and large created out of many ready-made components.

But many of the same questions arise. How will mass customisation and co-design affect the architectural design process? Will consumers and end-users be able to have a greater say and input? How will the choices be explained to them? What will be the balance between configured and free choices? In effect, how much more of a building can be economically designed-to-order rather than specified off the shelf? What should designers do with this potential for variety? And how will they, or should they, interact with the end-users and consumers of architecture, however they are defined, who may soon be co-designers? How will designers take the lead in all of this?

Perhaps there needs to be a clearer rallying cry. We used to live in a world in which most things had to be made to be the same, but we are about to enter a new era where, if we want it, many things – or perhaps all things – can be different. Δ

Towards an Animated Architecture Against Architectural Animation

Is there a danger that the medium has become the message? Is the employment of animatory techniques a triumph of style over substance? Neil Spiller, best known for his evangelising of new technologies and as an advocator of cyberspace, argues that an all-too-eager appropriation of animation software from other industries is leading architects to abandon a rigorous approach to architectural space in favour of a fetishisation of surface imagery.

SKETCHES

As someone who sees hundreds, perhaps thousands, of student portfolios a year, I can say I experience a deep sense of despair when a student produces a video machine or snaps open a CD-ROM tray instead of tabling drawings I can touch, feel and explore with my virtual imagination. My problem with architectural animations and the interminable boredom implicit in them is the fact that they often divert their creator from their primary task of creating architectural space.

Why should someone like me, who spends much of his time being evangelical about the benefits of technology to the practice of architecture, despise these attempts to communicate? It is because animations camouflage the uniqueness that each of us designers has. Instead of the virtual being groped for and approached by inner vision and the moving pencil, it has become static in order to be animated. Pinned down and then moving round in imitation of a creative act which has been abandoned before it has begun. It is a triumph of style over substance: in other words, the medium really has become the message.

As Sheep T Iconoclast said at a recent meeting at which I was present: 'I told you to photograph a building, would you immediately hire a helicopter and spiral around it?' For

thousands of years humanity has been viewing objects and events from a single point of view and imagined other viewpoints and possibilities. What are we really replacing this one-point perspective with? Nothing but chaos is the result of such visual hubris. Often one is frustrated by the voyeuristic fetishism that accompanies the opening of a box, or the dropping of an undercarriage, in animations. The aesthetic seems to be concerned with unwrapping or revealing the exterior of forms and not with their innate spatial and material constitution. Equally, one is irritated and nonplussed by coagulating blobs, wispy cyberplasm and trains of text or numbers travelling past one from shallow to deep screen. This tactic, used by *Star Wars*, betrays a vacuity similar to that of the film. Commonly, such work is accompanied by inane justification and sophist argument that is easily massacred outside the rarefied atmosphere of the academy. Techno soundtracks actively contribute to a condition that is akin to mental chewing gum. Chewing is about lassitude and stupor and everything being the same as everything else.

Obviously those who create animations of architecture are limited by the newness of the medium and the fact that much software is designed for industries other than architecture. The appropriation of software has caused many practitioners to press all the buttons simultaneously, or layer a million filters on top of one another for pure unadulterated effect. Such software is conceived to depict surfaces or

Previous page
Vectorial analysis – a section
through Croc-World

Above
Spitting form from the
maypole in savage ceremony.

Opposite
Object beside itself.

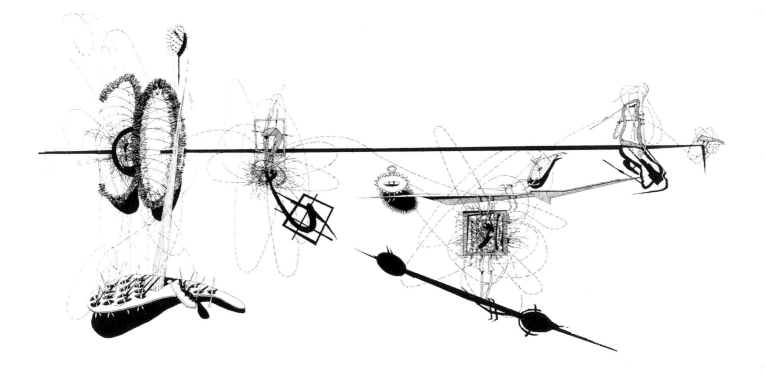

graphics that have little to do with the modalities of architectural production. This would be all well and good if architectural space could be depicted in these terms, but unfortunately it can't. Our technologised spacescape is highly complex, partial and vacillating; it exists right across a continuum of continuums – the virtuality continuum, the technological continuum, the inorganic – organic continuum and the electromagnetic continuum being but four of an infinite menu of spatial conditions available for the architect to choreograph. This is how architecture is becoming animated and it has little to do with architectural animation. Little spatial insight is gained from either anally transcribing the mechanical, jolty movements of a metallic armature into the sleek, nonrusty world of cyberspace or creating jointless, semitransparent virtual ghosts of an actual building. All in the hope of seducing a client to pay you to build its real-world deformed and rugged half-brother.

The technology of the virtual and its entire incredible trickle-down applications must be woven into actual architecture. This is where the 'anima' in animation should reside.

Current architectural animation often negates the enigma in architecture; everything has to be known in detail before it can be pushed into the virtual. This tactic alone betrays a crucial aspect of architectural creativity. Enigma is a creative tool that allows designers to see bifurcated outcomes in their sketches and drawings; it plays on the inability of drawings to faithfully record the distinct placement and extent of architectural elements. So one can see that the architectural drawing's status is still unquestioned when it comes to its most important function. This is why books are always more successful than films. They provide the enigmatic glimpse, the suggestion through a patina or sfumato and the half-seen and half-remembered; they allow the reader's imaginative construction of what is possibly an unworkable space imbued with personal association. The reason why few adaptations of books for the screen are successful is that books are fundamentally different to films.

Architectural design is fundamentally different to film theory and coercing one to become the other is erroneous. The specificity of much animation loses out to the more fluid multiple-viewpoint 'snapshot in time' drawing that has an imagined past and an imagined future. While this problem remains and, let's face it, it is likely to remain, I will advocate the use of drawn work to posit highly dynamic, networked and vacillating environments. Besides, an architect's personal touch is a critical marketing tool; to animate is often to dilute the difference between one architect and another. Something the Americans might like to consider. ⌂

All images are by Neil Spiller; photographs by Chris Bigg @ V23.

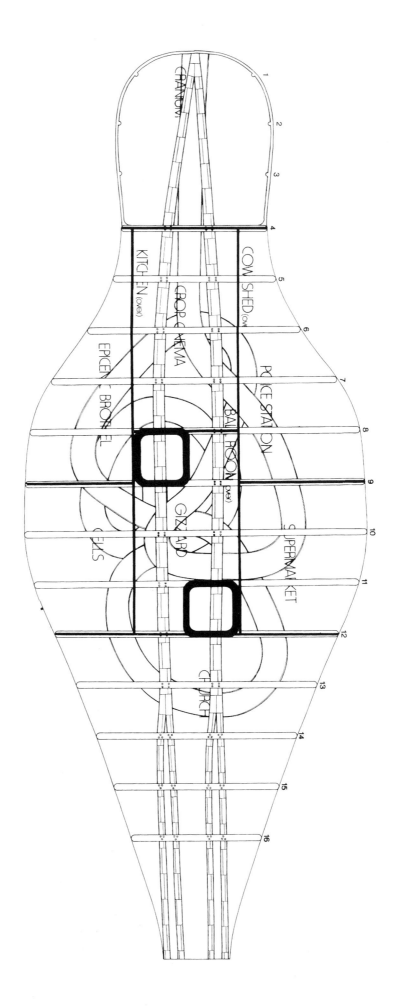

Back Off — or Back It Up!

Ben Nicholson has on a number of occasions been tempted to play Mary Shelley to his own Frankenstein, producing drawings of anthropomorphic buildings and an animated CD-ROM. Here he ponders his preference for breathing life into architecture rather than heavy-handed Mannerist contortions, while also considering the prospect of deliberately unanimated design.

'The INANIMATE thing is, to put it simply, orphaned, incomplete, and good for nothing, unless there be an animating soul to make use of it.'
Plutarch, *Moralia V*, The E at Delphi 390E

If a silent smile passes across a face, lighting it up as it goes, can we call the face animated any more, now that the motofilmic CAD boys have stampeded across our silent pleasures? Surely animation is about breathing life into something, rather than contorting the body architect into poses for which it is not well suited. Animators have for centuries tried to breathe life into bodies, creating the up-down heaving of the chest that signals that tomorrow is still on the menu. Air that goes in dry and cool and comes out warm and moist is an inside-out turn-on. There is a hair's breadth difference between full-blown halitosis and the minute eddies blowing from the lover's heart; both are proof of animation, but one is rank and the other personifies sweetness.

Any number of attempts at making homunculi, Adam Kadmons, golems, Frankenstein monsters and cybots posing as robo-sapiens have surely warned us to 'Back off!' from having a private go at animating the unanimatable. I am ashamed to say that I, too, have dabbled, in my feeble attempts to make bodies into buildings, to wit, the palandromic urinator standing within the Travulgar Square scheme of 1976. In the AA days of my education I was seduced by Lequeu's cow, on page 196 of *Visionary Architecture*, (Boullee, Ledeu, Lequeu, Houston, 1968) and made an overnight dash to Paris from London on a beat-up bike (31 hours) to see his watercolours first-hand. They were mesmerising, all the more so because of the scripted animations which, I later learned, were penned by Duchamp, the other teacher of animation in my career. A move to Philadelphia 10 years later, to live beside the grand fund of Duchamp, opened my eyes to that misanthropic practitioner of animation: this time the influence was all the more deadly, for his gases, sieves and emanations of The Large Glass diffused across my drawing table and keyboard to form my last and nastiest attempt to make a body architecture: the LOAF House.

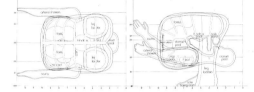

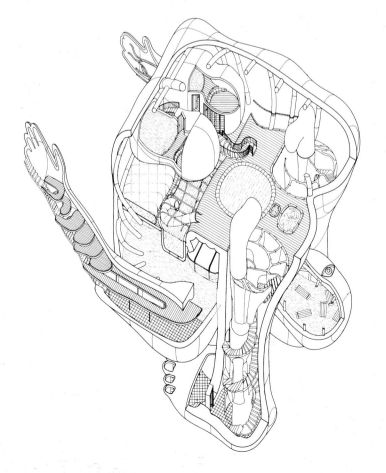

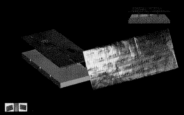
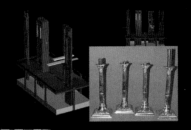

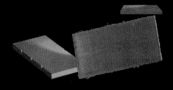
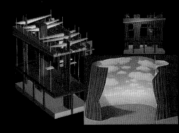
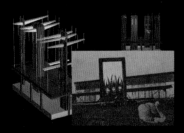
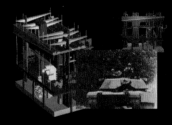
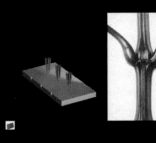
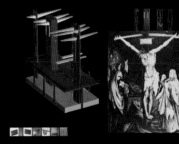
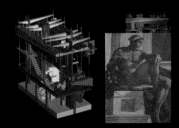

The grandest attempt at making a body animate, the LOAF House never saw the light of day, being permanently bound within the spinning plastic of a CD-ROM ($19.95 at www.pabooks.com). It was the epitome of hubris: my demand that something come to life, using all the creature comforts that HTML had to offer in 1996. The visitor can still be dragged about the house on the tail of a mouse, frogmarched in double-duty, quick time through passages, up stairs and down fireman's poles. The house is even animated through the eyes of a mosquito that flits from the leg of someone having dinner, flies up through a hole in the ceiling and sucks more blood out of someone else's thigh while they brush their teeth in the bathroom. The fabric of the LOAF house is little more than the underclothing of a desire to be alive. Perhaps its best expression is the 120 links to websites, etched irrevocably into the CD, most of which are now dead and gone. Making a project that actually witnesses its own digital death is perhaps the best contribution to the wish to animate something.

Having pledged to myself to not do anything beyond two dimensions until my 50th birthday, as a prison sentence for my own hubris, I live in crimped bonsai

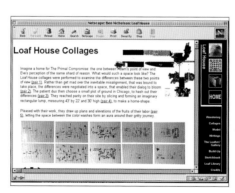

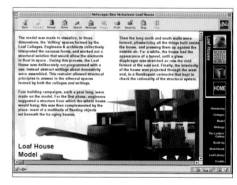

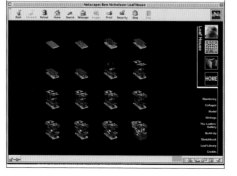

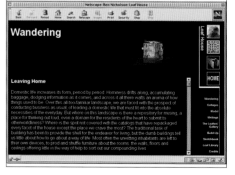

space, watching *The Birdman of Alcatraz* over and over again, doodling in a sketchbook amidst webs of lines and numbers (bennicholson.com), formulating a practice that is not the slightest bit impressed by the vanity of animation.

What pleasure it would be to contribute to a way of work that decried the avocation of Koolhausian rampancy, and made do with the simple joy of standing still in your own puddle of tears, no longer possessed by possessions but surrounded by a thing that is singularly unimpressed by the production of appliances and all that conjures up.

On a recent visit to the Native American city of Cahokia in southern Illinois, which was inhabited by 20,000 people in 1,500 (more than in London at the time), I stood at the bottom of an earthen mound whose base covers 14 acres and reaches over 100 feet high. It was made by transporting 15 million baskets of earth, each weighing 50 pounds. Now here's the question: would-you-rather carry earth baskets all day up a hill for something known to be unknown; or

would-you-rather sew cloth androids in China for McDonald's Happy Meals, for $1.50 a day, in the service of spoiled brats who momentarily thrill at ripping open the plastic bag, only to have that interest come crashing down after a sugar rush the size of a 48 oz Coke? 'Better is a handful with quiet, than two handfuls with toil, and a chasing after wind.'

What would an architecture look like that was deliberately not animated, but instead was filled with its own unbearable silence? Would the quiet be so loud that visitors rush out of the space with their hands clasped to their ears, screaming with the pain of emptiness? What would it take to make a building whose brief was to tear consumers away from the shopping carts, and take them to a place whose only task was to induce simple delight in the ordinary? At a recent meeting of Chicago's Architecture Club a prominent architect sat slumped in a chair, eyes welling, begging for the economic boom to end. Perhaps at this point in the game the only worthwhile brief left for us to contemplate is to make a building whose purpose is to bring about the shedding of tears (that is, if we can remember how to cry). ∆

All images are by Ben Nicholson. Peter Ippolito was the chief designer for those on pp 89 and 91.

Biographies

Mark Burry
Mark Burry occupies the Chair of Architecture and Building at Deakin University in Melbourne, Australia. He is a practising architect with an interest in realising 'difficult buildings' without compromising design intent. Since 1979 he has been Consultant Architect to the foundation who commissioned Antoni Gaudi to design the Sagrada Familia Church in Barcelona in 1882. Burry's role has included unravelling the mysteries of Gaudi's use of second order geometry (ruled surface) for the nave design. e-mail: mburry@deakin.edu.au

Tim Crayton
Tim Crayton is a consultant and writer on marketing and design. He is currently working on a PhD on the design and marketing implications of mass customisation, in the Department of Design at Brunel University. e-mail: Tim.Crayton@Brunel.ac.uk

Tim Durfee
Tim Durfee is on the design faculty at SCI-Arc (Southern California Institute of Architecture), co-founder of R/D Architecture and partner in Durfee Regn Sandhaus, a multidisciplinary design studio that produces digital interfaces, museum exhibitions and architecture. e-mail: durfeee@sciarc.edu

Pia Ednie-Brown
Pia Ednie-Brown teaches at the School of Architecture and Design at the Royal Melbourne Institute of Technology (RMIT), lecturing in design, theory and digital communications. She has recently returned to this teaching position after a year doing research for Telstra, the Australian telecommunications company, in a multi-disciplinary research team. She has acted as visiting critic and/or given lectures at ETH, Zurich, the TU, Berlin, Columbia University, Ljubljana University and Melbourne University. e-mail: pia@iii.rmit.edu.au

Mark Goulthorpe of dECOI
The dECOI atelier was created by Mark Goulthorpe in 1991 as a forward-looking architectural practice, whose design calibre was quickly established through winning entries in several international competitions, and with awards from various cultural institutions around the world. This has been reinforced by numerous publications, international lectures and conferences, and frequent guest-professorships, including a design unit at the renowned Architectural Association in London and the Ecole Speciale in Paris. e-mail: decoi@easynet.fr

Greg Lynn
Greg Lynn has taught throughout the United States and Europe and is presently the Professor of Spatial Conception and Exploration at the eth in Z̧rich, the Davenport Visiting Professor at Yale University and a studio professor at the University of California, Los Angeles. His office, Greg Lynn form, is working in collaborative partnerships with a variety of architects and designers on a range of projects. They include: the Uniserve Corporate Headquarters in Los Angeles; a line of international showrooms for pglife.com; the Cincinnati Country Day School in Cincinnati, Ohio; the Vision Plan for Rutgers University in New Brunswick, NJ; a book-container design for *Visionaire Magazine*; and the recently completed Korean Presbyterian Church of New York in New York City. His work has been exhibited internationally in both architecture and art museums and galleries. e-mail: node@glform.com   web: www.glform.com/

Gregory More
Gregory More is an architect/student based in Melbourne. He completed his undergraduate education at Victoria University of Wellington, New Zealand. Currently he is undertaking a Masters of Architecture at Deakin University, Australia, as part of which he has worked for the Paris-based firm dECOI. In recent years he has developed animations with Mark Burry for the Sagrada Familia in Barcelona and has received international recognition for his animation work. His current research examines the perceptual and technical implications of animation and variation within architectural design processes. e-mail: gregory_more@yahoo.com, gmore@deakin.edu.au

Ben Nicholson
Ben Nicholson teaches at the Illinois Institute of Technology, Chicago. His design work includes *Appliance House* (MIT Press, 1990) and *Loaf House* (1997, cd-rom from renaissancesociety.com). As part of a long-standing interest in American culture, he recently contributed to Bitomsky's documentary film *B-52* (2001). His current project is a book, *The Hidden Geometric Pavement in Michelangeloís Laurentian Library*, that muses over the nature of number, geometry and the structure of knowledge (2004). e-mail: comma@suba.com

Kas Oosterhuis
Professor at the Technical University in Delft, Oosterhuis is principal of Oosterhuis.nl in Rotterdam. Founder and Chairman of the Attitla Foundation in Rotterdam, he has also worked as unit master at the Architectural Association in London. Recent realised work include: Mult-media Pavilion Noord-Holland, Floriade; TTmonument Assen (with Ilona Lenard); 66 Houses 8bit Lelystad; The Headquarters for True Colours, Utrecht; and Bloemenwiede Ypenburg Nootdorp Sports Centre. e-mail: oosterhuis@oosterhuis.nl   web: www.oosterhuis.nl

Ali Rahim
Ali Rahim is the guest editor of Contemporary Processes in Architecture, *Architectural Design*, vol 70, no 3, 2000. He is principal of Ali Rahim Architecture in New York City and currently teaches at the University of Pennsylvania in Philadelphia. e-mail: alirahim@rcn.com   web: www.alirahimarchitecture.com

Christopher Romero
Christopher Romero is a studio professor and thesis adviser in the Graduate Program of Design and Technology at Parsons School of Design. He is also the director of Studio 313/OscillationNYC with his design partner Brian Kralyevich in the OscillationSF studio. e-mail: cromero@interport.net   web: www.oscillation.com

Neil Spiller
Neil Spiller is Director of the Diploma/M.Arch (Architecture) course at the Bartlett School of Architecture, University College London. He is the author of the monograph *Maverick Deviations* (Wiley-Academy, 1999) and of *Digital Dreams* – the Architecture of the New Alchemic Technologies (Ellipsis, 1998). He is also co-author with Peter Cook of *The Power of Contemporary Architecture* (Wiley-Academy, 1999). He has guest-edited several titles of *Architectural Design: Young Blood* (2000), *Architects in Cyberspace II* (1998) and *Integrating Architecture* (1996), and co-edited Architects in Cyberspace (1995). He is also the author of *Lost Architectures* (Wiley-Academy, 2000). Known around the world for his work with soft and digital technologies he is one of the original 'transarchitects', alongside Marcos Novak, Greg Lynn, Bernard Cache and Neil Denari. e-mail: spiller.jones@virgin.net

Bernard Tschumi
Bernard Tschumi is the Principal of Bernard Tschumi Architects, with offices in New York and Paris. Past projects include Parc de la Villette in Paris (1995), Le Fresnoy National Studio for Contemporary Arts in Tourcoing (1998) and the Lerner Hall Student Center in New York (1999). Since 1988 he has been Dean of the Graduate School of Architecture, Planning and Preservation at Columbia University in New York. He is also the author of Event Cities, The Manhattan Transcripts (1994), La Case Vide (1986), Cinegramme Folie (1987) and Architecture and Disjunction (1994). e-mail: nyc@tschumi.com web: www.tschumi.com

1941 AD Remembered 75

Monica Pidgeon has the final word in the last part of the *Architectural Design* history series – paying tribute to her staff, particularly Theo Crosby (1925–94). As the editor of ⅅ for almost 30 years (1946–75), Monica Pidgeon has had an almost inestimable influence on ⅅ. She shaped it as a magazine during the 40s, 50s and 60s, and oversaw its transfer to a book economy in the early 70s. Her recollections of her years at ⅅ read like a distilled history of 20th-century architecture: active in CIAM in the 40s and 50s; she visited South America in the 60s; and was entertained by Bucky Fuller at the Expo 67 in Montreal.

I first saw ⅅ (then *Architectural Design & Construction*) in the late 30s when I met Tony FE Towndrow, the editor. I remember whole issues on a single subject: office blocks, housing and hospitals. And a boring brick-red cover with an advertisement in the middle. In her overview of ⅅ Jan Stratford has explained how I came to be involved later: first ghosting for Tony during the war and then taking over as editor in 1946 when he left for Australia.[1]

I want to pay tribute to the wonderful people who worked for me. First it was Barbara Randell, Tony's ex-secretary, who showed me the ropes of running a magazine, how to process copy, deal with the printers and so on. She and I had a great time together for eight years but our bosses, Messrs Dottridge and Moss, the founders and directors of the Standard Catalogue Co, did not like the idea of a woman in charge of their magazine, even though I had a diploma from the Bartlett. A list of male architects' names on the masthead as 'consultants' was the solution.

Since Ireland had not been involved in the war, Barbara and I went to Dublin for a week to seek material for a special Irish ⅅ. But every architect we visited immediately took us out for a drink or meal and couldn't be persuaded to talk shop. It remained for our friend Noel Moffet to act as guest editor and he later brought all the copy to us in a holdall, together with bottles of alcohol our friends had asked us to bring them but which customs had confiscated and held for us in Dublin Castle.

Soon after this I was in Lausanne for the birth of the Union Internationale des Architectes (UIA). Patrick Abercrombie was voted president and Jean Tschumi (father of Bernard) was one of the founders. I saw my first Le Corbusier building, the Maison de Verre in Geneva. I can't remember whether it was before or after this that I went to Stockholm, as usual in search of material for the magazine, and met Ralph Erskine who had been trapped in Sweden by the war and seemed already to be half-Swedish.

Towards the end of the 40s, the CIAM (Congress Internationaux d'Architecture Moderne) held its first postwar conference in Bridgwater, Somerset, where I was very thrilled to meet luminaries like Le Corbusier, Josep Lluis Sert, Jacob Bereud Bakema, Siegfried Giedion, Cornelis van Eesteren and Walter Gropius.

I helped to organise the next CIAM meeting, at Hoddesdon in Hertfordshire, and again met all these stars. I think the theme was 'transportation'. Le Corbusier was particularly impressive one morning when, at the end of an inconclusive debate, he rose, saying 'il me semble que', and, with his coloured pencils and large sheets of paper, solved the problem within minutes. It was 1951, the year of the Festival of Britain, so we took the delegates to the South Bank.

Ernö Goldfinger and his wife invited me to drive with them to the 1953 CIAM meeting in Aix-en-Provence.

Top row, left to right
Monica Pidgeon's predecessor **Tony FE Towndrow**, editor of △ 1932–46.

A photograph of **Barbara Randell** in 1952. Tony Towndrow's ex-secretary, Randell taught Pidgeon a great deal about publishing.

Theo Crosby, 1961. Technical editor 1953–62 and a founding member of Pentagram.

Ken Frampton on a train in Germany, 1964. Now Ware

Professor in Architecture at Columbia University, New York, Frampton was technical editor 1962–64.

Bottom row, left to right
Robin Middleton, 1965. Technical editor 1965–72.

Photograph of **Monica Pidgeon**, 1960s.

Peter Murray, 1972. Murray was with the magazine from 1969 to 1973. He first joined as assistant art editor and then replaced Middleton as technical editor.

Right
The Centresoyus Building by Le Corbusier in Moscow, 1958. The Russian authorities did not rate it and only allowed Monica Pidgeon to visit it after she had met the architect who oversaw the construction. It was dilapidated and the interior was painted a dirty green and dark brown.

Above and far right
Niemeyer's sensuous concrete curves in Brasilia: the presidential palace and the bones of the cathedral.

This was even more memorable both intellectually and socially and ended, fittingly, with a party on the roof of Le Corbusier's Unité d'Habitation in Marseilles. But the French organisers put on a nude cabaret and several of the delegates protested and walked out. It was at Aix that I first met the Smithsons.

Just after this Barbara left $\triangle$ and Theo Crosby joined us. We coined the title 'technical editor' for him and I enjoyed eight exciting years working with him. Alas, he is no longer alive to tell the tale himself, so I must speak for him ...

His influence was immense. In those days we ran the magazine from late morning into the evening, as described by Ken Frampton, so Theo started his day doing sculpture at St Martins School of Art and also found time to build himself a house in Hammersmith Lower Mall.[2] He persuaded our bosses to let him design the magazine covers instead of using an advertisement. (I recently saw some of these on sale in a London gallery.) He got artists to do designs on special paper which was bound into $\triangle$, the first being by Eduardo Paolozzi. Theo also designed a lovely wrapper for a book we did on modern houses from material already published in $\triangle$.

In parallel with working on AD he was always involved with other related activities. For example, to show off the capabilities of our printing arm, Whitefriars Press, he started a little magazine called Upper Case which ran into five editions before our directors axed it on grounds of cost. These are now art collectors' items.

In 1956 Theo dreamed up the idea for the subsequently famous exhibition 'This is Tomorrow' at the Whitechapel Gallery in east London, for which he organised artists and architects to work together in groups. He also put on an exhibition on Le Corbusier at the Building Centre in London and financed it by selling a limited number – 100 pages – of advertisements in the catalogue at £100 each (quite a lot in those days). We sold these within a few days and firms offered us bribes to increase the number.

Theo and I went together to Expo 58 in Brussels and were impressed by Egon Eiermann's German Pavilion, Sverre Fehn's Scandinavian pavilion and Le Corbusier and Charles Xenakis's pavilion for Philips. That same year the UIA chose Moscow for its venue and we were received by Viktor Khrushchev in St George's Hall in the Kremlin, and lodged in the wedding-cake-like Ukraine Hotel. For tours we split into language groups which were in the charge of charming Intourist students. Because we had VIP status, we did not have to join the mile-

long queue to visit Lenin's tomb in Red Square. We did manage to do quite a lot of wandering on our own and visited parts of the Kremlin and the impressive covered shopping centre Gum. Some of us got to see Le Corbusieris Centresoyus Building with its project architect Kolli, who later became $\triangle$'s Russian correspondent.

I had gradually collected foreign correspondents in many countries – architects I had met and whose work I admired. They proved to be wonderful contacts. Thus, going to and from Moscow, I was shown round Helsinki and Copenhagen by two of them. It was they, too, who were the authors of the city map-guides we published. Hans Hollein did the one on Vienna.

In 1961 the UIA congress was held in London and $\triangle$ was much involved. The Queen Elizabeth Hall on the South Bank had been hired for it and Theo designed a beautiful members' pavilion nearby. He persuaded Taylor Woodrow to build it for free; Ernest Race to contribute seating (which Theo had designed); and artists like John McHale and Edward Wright to decorate the fence. Theo also produced an illustrated catalogue of all the contributing delegates' work, printed by Whitefriars.

I was on the committee for the UK congress and was allotted the social organisation. vips were invited to a Guildhall gala evening. Among them was Buckminster Fuller and, while dancing with me, he complained at not being an invited speaker. So I invited him. On the dot of nine o'clock next morning, he turned up and launched his long-cherished dream, the 'World Design Science Decade'. The upshot was that $\triangle$ published his manifesto, had it translated into many languages and mailed it to all the uia secretariats. From then on we maintained close contact with Bucky and published his work and ideas. At Expo 67 in Montreal the high spot was being shown round his famous dome by him and then dining with his family and colleagues.

It was as a result of Theo's collaboration with Taylor Woodrow that they seduced him away from $\triangle$ to work on a huge development and Ken Frampton assumed the mantle of technical editor. He has already described his time with $\triangle$.[3] Certainly, he introduced more serious and critical writing.

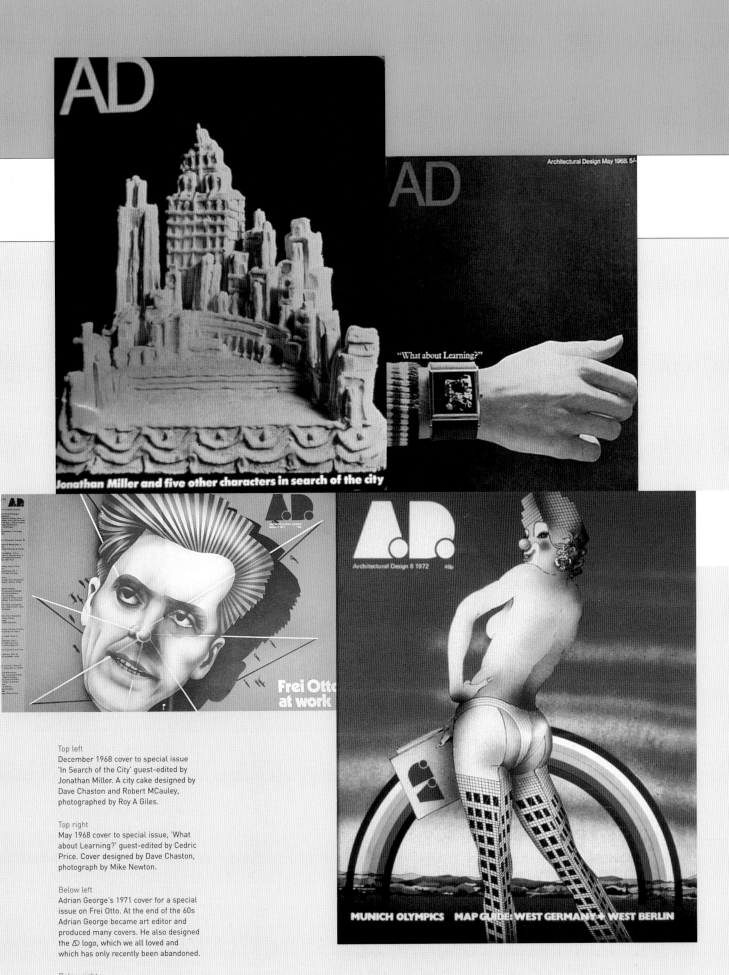

Top left
December 1968 cover to special issue
'In Search of the City' guest-edited by
Jonathan Miller. A city cake designed by
Dave Chaston and Robert MCauley,
photographed by Roy A Giles.

Top right
May 1968 cover to special issue, 'What
about Learning?' guest-edited by Cedric
Price. Cover designed by Dave Chaston,
photograph by Mike Newton.

Below left
Adrian George's 1971 cover for a special
issue on Frei Otto. At the end of the 60s
Adrian George became art editor and
produced many covers. He also designed
the AD logo, which we all loved and
which has only recently been abandoned.

Below right
The August 1972 cover by Adrian George.

In 1963 Ken was left in charge while I went away for the first time, for nine weeks. My parents lived in Chile and had invited me to visit them. So I took the opportunity to stop over in various places. In Rio de Janeiro, Lucio Costa showed me the exuberant architecture of Oscar Niemeyer and the Roberto brothers, and Sergio Bernardes, who was planning the extension of the city, entertained me in his beautiful home perched on a rocky promontory overlooking the ocean. In Brasìlia, I was bowled over by Niemeyer's sensuous work: the palace, the government buildings and the cathedral. There had been a political upheaval and armed soldiers paraded everywhere.

The scene was similar in Buenos Aires – another political upheaval. But I managed to see some good modern building and to meet Amancio Williams, and Clorindo Testa and his talented young team.

In Santiago, Sersio Gonzalez and Jorge Poblete had just completed their prize-winning stadium (which Pinochet used in 1973 to round up left-wing 'undesirables') and Sergio Larrain and Carlos Garcia Huidobro had built a large and impressive housing estate – all featured later in $\triangle$.

I spent five weeks in Chile, seeking my roots after an absence of 30 years, and was loath to leave but went on to Peru. It was in Lima that John Turner took me to see the *barriadas* (shantytowns) that surround the city, mile upon mile of them in the desert. I had never seen anything like it and was appalled. But John had been making a social study of them and I vowed to publish it in $\triangle$. This we did, with his and Pat Crookes' help, and the UN followed it up with a film.

In Bogota I met an old friend, German Samper, who had worked on Chandigarh in Le Corbusier's office in Paris but was now head of a large and prosperous practice. Architecture in Colombia was straightforward Modern - they called it *sobrio*, sober. One of the country's best architects at the time was Rogelio Samona. I stayed with the architect Alex Bright, an $\triangle$ correspondent who later became head of the world-famous Gold Museum. It was interesting to see how contemporary architecture differed in each South American country.

It is sad that our next technical editor, Robin Middleton, has not cared to contribute to this series of articles, because the period when he was with $\triangle$ (1964 to 1971) was one of great change, as Peter Murray outlines in his article.[4] Robin commissioned several thoughtful issues from Roy Landua; 'Team Ten Primer' from the Smithsons, a sequel to ciam which they had helped to kill; 'The Heroic Age', also by them

with a follow-up by Robin about its presents. And then there was '2000 +', compiled by John McHale, which attempted to communicate the idea of technological innovation to an architecture that was still largely hidebound by a vision of the fine arts. Cedric Price edited a forward-looking issue emphasising new ideas about 'learning' as opposed to 'teaching'.

The December issue was always given over to a 'special'. 'Team Ten Primer' was one of these. So was Jonathan Miller's 'In Search of the City' in which he aimed to show how the image of the city has flourished as an imaginative metaphor. There were also two fascinating Japanese issues by Gunther Nitsche: 'Ma' and 'Binding'.

Peter Murray joined us in 1969 as art editor. He took over as technical editor when Robin left in 1971 and stayed till 1973. It was during their overlap that a dramatic change took place. $\triangle$'s publishers were now part of a larger organisation who wanted to liquidate the magazine. We were given two months to quit. However, I persuaded Basil Dotteridge and Malcolm Moss, our directors, not to withdraw support entirely but to let us change to a 'book economy' (no advertisements), reduce size and paper quality, and find an off-set printer in place of our expensive hot-metal one.

From being an anxious period, it became an exciting time with a four-colour printing process to experiment with. $\triangle$ ceased to be a glossy magazine. We now focused our attention much more on the future, on new and alternative technology, on energy conservation, on planning flexibility. The avant-garde magazine that we became was loved by the young.

But the financial support from the publishers was less than lukewarm. So, though loath to leave $\triangle$, I accepted the RIBA's offer to edit their journal. Having enjoyed every minute of what Ken has called 'the non-stop merry-go-round of production, the heady days ... with never a dull moment', I quit in November 1975, leaving Martin Spring and Haig Beck in my place. $\triangle$

Monica Pidgeon stayed with the RIBA for three and a half years before starting her own company, Pidgeon Audio Visual, to publish mini-audio illustrated lectures with well-known architects and other designers talking about their work and ideas. They sell internationally to the academic world. The enterprise is ongoing.

Left
Variations on Adrian George's late 60s logo design, illustrating the power of its identity by the early 70s.

Bottom
Examples of pages from the Cosmorama section in the 70s after four-colour printing became available.

Notes
1. Jan Stratford, 'The Ideas Circus', *Architectural Design*, vol 70, no 2, 2000, pp 98-103.
2. Ken Frampton, 'AD in the 60s: A Memoir', *Architectural Design*, vol 70, no 3, 2000, pp 98-102.
3. Ibid.
4. Peter Murray, 'Zoom! Whizz! Pow!', *Architectural Design*, vol 70, no 4, 2000, pp 100-105.

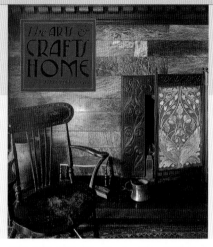

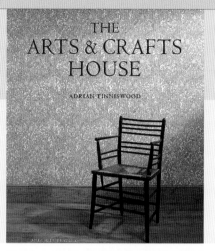

The Arts & Crafts Home, Wendy Hitchmough,
Pavilion (London), 2000, 192 pp, colour,
HB £30

The Arts & Crafts House, Adrian Tinniswood,
Mitchell Beazley/Octopus Publishing Group Ltd
(London), 1999, 176 pp, colour, HB £25

There is certainly no shortage of books about the Arts & Crafts Movement on the market, and recently, another two volumes have been added to the already vast canon. It has reached a point where so much has been written on the subject that it is difficult to find new ground that has yet to be covered; but one of the publications in the spotlight here does add significantly to the study of this field.

The Arts & Crafts Home approaches its subject from a completely new angle, and is the product of the exceptionally detailed cross-disciplinary research of Wendy Hitchmough, an accomplished architectural historian and author who manages to combine academicism and readability with apparent ease. Through an intimate portrait of life in the more liberated artistic houses of the 1860s to 1910s, it explains the whys and wherefores behind the contents of the interiors, examining both their stylistic sources and the influence of social factors on their form and placing within the context of each room setting.

The main chapters of the book each tackle a different domain of the Arts & Crafts home: the entrance, the drawing room, the dining room, the service wing and the bedroom. These are complemented by two preliminary chapters explaining the planning of the Arts & Crafts house and providing background information on the development of the movement in Britain and America. Hitchmough effectively communicates the reasons behind the movement's differing manifestations in the two areas by alluding to their contrasting socio-economic and historical contexts.

The entire book is filled with references to a wide range of sources – from architectural and historical writings and many original archives, to contemporary novels and etiquette manuals – all of which enrich its quality and depth. Despite drawing from this vast resource, Hitchmough does not make the mistake of muddling her argument by illustrating it with too many examples: instead, she focuses on a few carefully selected houses, so that by the end of the book the reader has acquired both a broad knowledge of the period and a detailed acquaintance with these few important buildings and their contents. The book is further enriched by Martin Charles' exquisite photography. Excellent end matter includes detailed footnotes, a good select bibliography, and a list of houses to visit, with details of the opening arrangements and telephone numbers of each property.

Whilst *The Arts & Crafts Home* is a book that demands, and deserves, to be read from cover to cover, *The Arts & Crafts House* is one that can be more easily dipped into. Adrian Tinniswood's text is lively, anecdotal, sometimes journalistic, and is presented in easily digestible chapters complemented by a wealth of photographs whose captions effectively summarise the text they accompany, so that a quick glance will reveal the gist of the argument. The order of the chapters, however, is not as well considered as it might have been. Whilst broadly arranged into five sections – ostensibly covering the origins of the Arts & Crafts Movement in Morris &Co; architects' houses; the movement in America; the rural idyll; and the influence of Arts & Crafts on later stylistic developments – the contents of these sections sometimes overlap, and within them chapters giving historical background are interspersed somewhat randomly with detailed accounts of specific buildings. The occasional unattributed quotation will prove a frustration to the more enquiring reader, although this lack is to a certain extent compensated for by a good bibliography, and the index is well compiled. All things considered, this book, although it makes no contribution to scholarship on the Arts & Crafts Movement, would nevertheless provide a helpful and comprehensive introduction for the reader with little prior knowledge of the subject. Δ
Abigail Grater

Peter Karle and
Ramona Buxbaum

Karle/Buxbaum

The intellectual approach and working practices of many
architects are formulated during their architectural
education. **Torsten Schmiedeknecht** looks at the
work of Karle/Buxbaum, a small successful practice
in Darmstadt in Germany, who have developed the
conceptual base and design method of their college
years and applied it as a practical working philosophy.

*The 'bricoleur' is adept at performing a large number of diverse tasks; but, unlike the engineer,
he does not subordinate each of them to the availability of raw materials and tools conceived a
nd procured for the purpose of the project. His universe of instruments is closed and the rules
of his game are always to make do with 'whatever is at hand'* [1]

When I asked Peter Karle whether he considered
architecture to be an art or a science he stated that he thought
architecture was an applied art containing some scientific
aspects. To explain his point of view he cited Levi-Strauss'
definition of the bricoleur, quoted above, which illustrates
where Karle/Buxbaum come from intellectually but also
provides an orientation of where they stand professionally
as a practice with regard to their client base and the type
of work they do.

The two partners both trained at the Technische Hochschule
Darmstadt (now Technische Universität) at a time when Günter
Behnisch – one of the most successful postwar German
architects – and Max Bächer – one of the most notorious
judges in national and international competitions in Germany –
were the two most powerful influences in the school. Collage
City had just been published in English, and the first wave of
buildings that had been conceived with a critical notion of

modernism in mind had been erected in Germany,
when Peter Karle commenced his studies in
architecture in 1978. In the early 1980s, when Ramona
Buxbaum started her course, Kenneth Frampton and
his notion of Critical Regionalism were beginning
to have an impact on architectural education and by
then Robert Venturi's *Complexity and Contradiction
in Architecture* had been translated into German.

The introduction of metaphorical thinking as a tool
for architectural design, and the overcoming of the idea
of the metanarrative that had prevailed in the Modernist
philosophy of design, was leading to an opening
up of the architectural discussion. This partly found
its articulation in the stylistic expression of Post-
modernism at its height, but another effect was the
acknowledgement that architecture should become
a more open system, embedded in all walks of life and

culture and drawing its influences not just from within the architectural profession but also from these.

In the mid-1980s Peter Karle became familiar with Jean Baudrillard's 'Fatal Strategies' and in 1986 he introduced me to Jean Nouvel's 'Towards many Architectures – Anti-manifesto/parody in favour of a pluralistic architecture' which had been published in *L'Architecture d'Aujourd'Hui* in 1984:

> ...I am prepared to like them a lot: the pure and the impure, the virtuous and the whores, the spontaneous and the sophisticated, the naked and the all done up, the working-class and the bourgeois. As long as they are alive! I am horrified by the mummies and the resurrected; let's leave them to Frankenstein.
> As long as they are tolerant! Slave seeks mistress is not for me! ...I have a weakness for 'turned-on' ones: the ones that reflect the aesthetics of their times, influenced by literature, the comic-strips, TV, films, photo and artistic creation of their times ...

Karle/Buxbaum's design method has to be seen in relation to the developments that took place during the time of their architectural education. When they start the design work for a new job, in most cases the project is in due course given a nickname derived from the conceptual idea that drives it. This not only enables the partners to remind themselves constantly of what the project is or was about, but is also a continuation of the way they were both taught and have passed on their knowledge as teachers. The kindergarten project, for example, was internally named 'play or tool box' and the title served as a helpful constraint during the design and, most importantly, during the building phase. The metaphor is seen as a design tool and its application is aimed at the public's understanding of the individual scheme. Thus the architects try to signify content both programmatically and intellectually. Ramona Buxbaum told me of the moment in the design process for the project for 11 social-housing units when red and green Monopoly houses appeared on a desk in the office and references to the typology of the ordinary house were established.

In Karle/Buxbaum's present work the idea of the sign as architecture, as Venturi had articulated it, is being extended with a Minimalist approach that has its roots in contemporary Swiss architecture. A playful interpretation of the traditional theme of the 'gate' is still inherent in the concept of the Fire Station project, but the aesthetic articulation becomes more severe and serious than in earlier projects. But despite the more Minimalist touch of later projects the practice has not developed a house style, and refuses to do so. Every project is seen as a new starting point that provides

a new challenge and problem to be solved, whether this be functional, programmatical or visual in its nature.

The shift in the way architects are commissioned in Germany, especially with regard to the competition system, has caused a change in the economic strategy of Karle/Buxbaum. Neither of the partners had any backup or family connections and the usual 'first job or house for a relative' was never part of the practice's equation. Having participated successfully in more than 40 competitions and winning 15 prizes and commendations – among which were six first prizes – the practice has gained only two commissions as a direct result of competitions it has won. In the early 1990s the partners decided to approach local clients directly with their portfolio. The strategy proved to be very successful and their client list now comprises two housing associations and the local suppliers of electricity and public transport, and gas and water, as well as private clients.

If you look at the nature of the projects the practice is dealing with, its motto to 'playfully apply cunning tricks' becomes evident. Karle/Buxbaum see themselves as everyday architects dealing with the matrix rather than the monument. Their declared ambition is to produce an architecture that fits in with the given circumstances and is able to survive unnoticed as part of the city fabric, but one that can at the same time sustain an identity when critically analysed. Keeping the greater picture as a priority, Karle/Buxbaum's work is caringly detailed but the practice does not try to reinvent the wheel for the design of every new handrail. A maximum of one or two 'conceptual themes' are explored per project in order to keep things simple and in control. Time, money and client satisfaction are top of the priority list for the two partners: they understood very early on that this is the best way to stay in business, and that architecture is not just for architects.

Notes
1. Claude Levi-Strauss, *The Savage Mind*, Weidenfeld & Nicolson, (London) 1966, p 17. Quoted here from Colin Rowe and Fred Koetter, *Collage City*, MIT Press (Cambridge, Mass), paperback edition 1995, p 102.
2. Jean Nouvel 'Towards many Architectures – Anti-manifesto/parody in favour of a pluralistic architecture', *L'Architecture d'Aujourd'Hui*, 231, February 1984, p 11.

Fire Station,
Merck Chemical and Pharmaceutical Works,
Darmstadt, Germany, 1999–2000

The fire station is one of three on the Merck premises and consists of the conversion of three existing steel-frame buildings which are arranged in an L-shape around a generous yard. The station houses an operational area with an appliance hall for 10 fire engines, which faces east towards the yard. An amenities zone that provides accommodation and rest- and shower rooms is situated at the back of the appliance hall and faces west and north. One of the typical functional elements of every fire station, the gates of the appliance hall, were developed as the main visual feature of the building by replacing the complete eastern facade with new folding aluminium-framed GRP gates and fixed panels that stretch over the full height of the station. The GRP gates – which because of their lightweight construction can be operated manually – provide the appliance hall with daylight.

Two Houses Around a Courtyard, social housing, Darmstadt, Germany, 1995–98
This social-housing scheme was the first time that a won competition actually led to a commission for Karle/Buxbaum. The brief was to provide accommodation mainly for single parents. By arranging the 11 units into two buildings the practice kept in line with the suburban structure of the surrounding area, and also provided a central courtyard to be used by the occupants as a playground and meeting place. The aim was to enable the single parents to share duties and responsibilities for their children, and the courtyard was conceived as an exterior living room to the flats, all of which have visual contact with it.

Apart from kitchens and bathrooms, all the spaces in the individual units are of similar sizes and proportions and the occupants thus have a greater choice of how to inhabit their flats. All units provide both a corridor circulation and the possibility to interconnect rooms.

Karle/Buxbaum played with the idea of the image of the ordinary house for the scheme and elements like the pitched roof, the roof overhang and the porch are deliberately employed in order to achieve a building with which its occupants could identify.

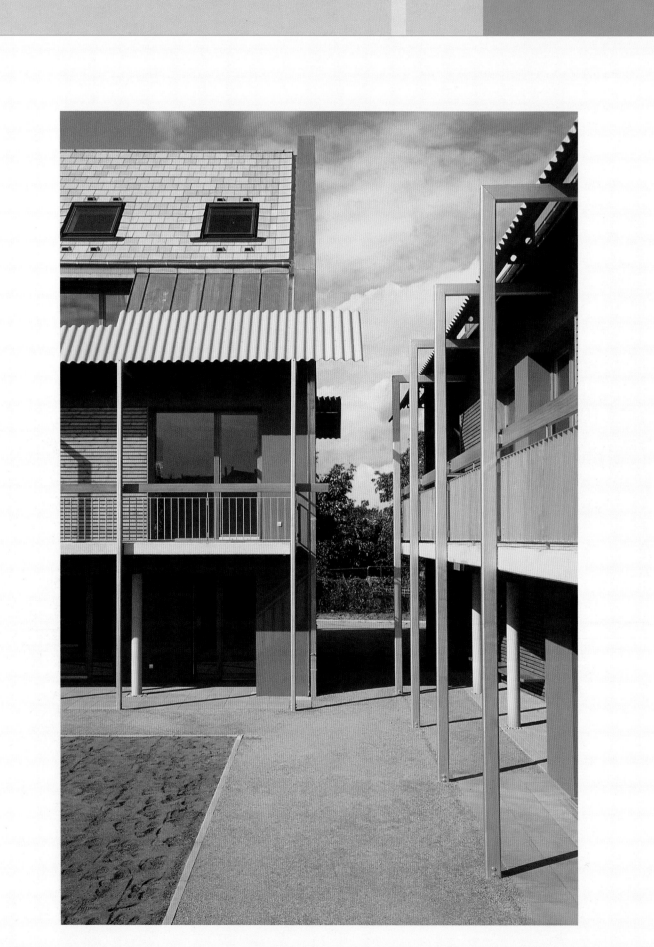

Kindergarten, Messel, Germany, 1994–97
Situated in a suburban setting outside Darmstadt and
containing spaces for three playgroups, a day-care room, a
multipurpose space, a kitchen and a self-contained flat, the
two-storey kindergarten was conceived as a 'play or toy box'.
The building has a north–south orientation with the playrooms
facing an open field on the south side of the site and the
service rooms accommodated in the north part of the building.
The external appearance is dominated by vertical timber
cladding. The south-facing facade consists of two layers, one
of which provides the physical boundary between internal and
external spaces. In front of this boundary is situated another
layer which defines the actual threshold between building
and field. This features a play terrace on the first floor from
which the children can access the garden via two stairs and
a slide. The threshold is articulated as a frame, containing
coloured blinds that provide shelter from the sun. A playful
interpretation of the brief, the project resists patronising the
young occupants with child-friendly imagery and leaves them
to explore their building in their own way. ⌂

The practice now employs six architects and four students. Between 1985 and 2000 six built
projects were awarded commendations and mentions, and the practice has won 15 prizes and
commendations, and mentions in national and international competitions.

1985   Peter Karle obtained his *Diplom Ingenieur Architektur* (Diploma in Architecture) at the Technische Universität Darmstadt. From 1987 to 1992 he was scientific assistant to Professor Hansjakob Führer at the Institute for Design and Industrial Building at the TU Darmstadt.

1988   In collaboration with I Schulze, Karle won second prize in a competition for a community centre in Friedrichsdorf near Frankfurt and first prize in a competition for a bank in Langen. He also won first prize in a competition for a town hall in Hirschberg. None of the schemes were commissioned.

1989   Ramona Buxbaum finished her studies and gained her Diplom Ingenieur Architektur at the Technische Universität Darmstadt. In 1994 she was scientific assistant to Professor Moritz Hauschild at the Institute for Design and Building Construction at the TU Darmstadt.

1990   The architectural practice P Karle/R Buxbaum was founded in Darmstadt.

1992   Two extensions to residential buildings were commissioned and were completed in 1993.

1993   Karle was awarded the Villa Massimo scholarship, the Prix de Rome of the Federal Republic of Germany. He spent one year in Rome working on his own architectural projects and exchanging experiences with other residential scholars such as the German photographer Thomas Ruff.

1995   The practice won first prize in a social-housing competition for 11 units in Darmstadt. The scheme, internally titled 'Two Houses Around a Courtyard', was completed in 1998 and gained two commendations.

1996   The technical coordination building for HEAG, the local electricity and public transport provider, was completed.

1997   The kindergarten in Messel opened on 5 September.

2000   The fire station for Merck Darmstadt was completed. Work started on the large-scale renovation of an Ernst Neufert Meisterbau housing scheme in Darmstadt. The practice also completed a building accommodating facilities to filter drinking water for the Südhessische Gas- und Wasser AG.

Site Lines

Rachel Armstrong, guest editor of the popular *Space Architecture* issue of *Architectural Design* (vol 70, no 2), takes a look at Massimiliano Fuksas's new design for the Italian Space Agency's headquarters in Rome.

The Italian Space Agency – Agenzia Spaziale Italiana (ASI) – is starting the third millennium by commissioning its new headquarters from the well-known architect Massimiliano Fuksas, who was president of the 2000 Architecture Biennale in Venice.

The ASI is a government agency, founded in 1988. It was set up to promote, coordinate and manage national programmes and bilateral and multilateral cooperation programmes, and to promote and support Italian scientific and industrial participation in the European Space Agency (ESA) programmes, in harmonisation with national ones. It is organised in four operating areas: scientific research (ars); technical area for applicable programmes; strategical and funding; and legal and administrative.

The new headquarters will embrace all the departments of the ASI and will be constructed over 6,500 square metres in the former Montello military barracks in Via Guido Reni, in the Flaminio district in Rome. Significantly, the now abandoned barracks is developing into a cultural district, a setting for remarkable new examples of architecture such as Renzo Piano's auditorium, which is currently under construction. The remainder of the barracks has been set aside for the Centre for Contemporary Arts, designed by Zaha Hadid, winner of the related international design competition in 1998.

Unusually, part of the brief required the architect not only to consider the building's professional function but also its relationship with the future Centre for Contemporary Arts. In doing so, Fuksas has produced the outward expression of new futuristic space ambitions in Italy rather than giving an old military institution a face-lift.

Fuskas's radical solution was to design a unique building that appears to represent a giant cell at first glance. From a distance, the elevations convey a regular, geometric complex but the outer covering has a transparent section that reveals an undulating, organic nucleus of corridors and public spaces which are presented in a way that makes the building's interior look as though it is undulating like cell cytoplasm. This organism-like entity is a unique blend of art and science that has created a dialogue between many conventionally polar disciplines, and Fuskas has devised structural and conceptual schemes to break down the barriers between the two dominions. His design examines the occupation of architectural space from physical (scientific) and symbolic (artistic) perspectives, stimulating a cross-fertilisation that will ultimately benefit both disciplines. Ultimately his new vision will be manifest as part of the first space programmes scheduled for the new headquarters.

Through this innovative structure, Fuskas has opened a window to the future flow of human traffic that will inhabit space and the building will reflect the collaborative exploration of space that will occur at the headquarters. The way in which he has rethought boundaries that conventionally exist between ideas and matter predicates the changes we will experience when space travel becomes increasingly accessible to the research and public communities.

Ultimately ASI's winning choice embodies the new challenges that humans will face when they take their first steps into orbit. Just as our way of looking at the world will have to evolve, expand and embrace new frontiers as we boldly go into the extraterrestrial environment, so our understanding of the traditions of art and science will have to change. We will need to be more cooperative in every discipline of human thought and expression in order to make habitable environments and bring to life the first human space colonies. △

For further information see the ASI's website on www.asi.it

Highlights from Wiley-Academy

Neil Spiller

Lost Architectures

WILEY-ACADEMY

Peter Cook
The Bartlett School of Architecture, London:
'Neil Spiller is great in that he makes no attempt to conceal his enthusiasms and irritations beneath any layers of correctness, veneration or smart-quote ... Few of my friends can be this enthusiastic and this naughty. Yet underneath the bubbling and grungeing lies an architectural mind of pure silver and a hand of boiling black ink.'

Ben Nicholson
Illinois Institute of Technology, Chicago:
'Neil Spiller has never been afraid to articulate his beliefs and concerns ... [His] writings have become points of reference within both the academy and the profession, [and] have become a key part of the current discourse.'

LOST ARCHITECTURES
Neil Spiller – 'Most Out-There Theorist' in *Wallpaper** magazine (Richard Hinzel, July/August 2000)

It is often argued that the best architecture is built on compromise. Neil Spiller, the influential architect, writer and educator, takes the opposite view. In this, his latest book, he expounds the theory that many of the bravest and most original products of the architectural mind are to be found in projects which never came to fruition – pure dreams that remain untainted by constrictions of cost, commerce or conservatism.

Lost Architectures presents a selection of unbuilt projects from the last two decades of the 20th century. Most have seldom, if ever, been published before, and some represent the last hand-drawn work of their creators before the computer came to dominate the design of the built environment. Spiller has selected these projects on the basis that they were brave and inspiring at the time of their creation, and have remained so in the intervening years as truly inspirational work does not lose its power in the course of time. Whilst varying greatly in form and style, each embodies a spirit defined by Spiller as New Romanticism, which combines angular allusions to the machine age with a certain camp mannerism. Among the architects featured are Odile Decq and Benoît Cornette, Nigel Coates, Will Alsop and Peter Cook.

Spiller writes here with his customarily direct, accessible and humorous yet highly informed style. He is renowned for the originality of his own architectural work, as well as for his perceptive talent-spotting and nurturing of students

and budding architects who have demonstrated their own potential. His wide knowledge of the field and incisive writings earned him the title of 'Most Out-There Theorist' in *Wallpaper** magazine (July/August 2000), and his previous books and essays have been described by his contemporaries as holding 'iconic status' within architectural theory. *Lost Architectures* promises to make no less great an impression on the architectural world, providing a valuable point of reference for architects and students of architecture at every stage of their development, as well as for the lay reader.

This is an opportunity to glimpse some of the most exciting, yet hitherto hidden, work that has been produced by a broad range of architects, many of whom have since achieved recognition and acclaim, but some of whom remain in relative obscurity. It is also an essential document that preserves for posterity projects which might otherwise have been truly lost in the course of time.

PB 0 471 49535 2, £19.99; 279 x 217 mm;
128 pages; February 2001

FUTURE SYSTEMS

UNIQUE
BUILDING

LORD'S MEDIA CENTRE

WILEY-ACADEMY

Stirling Prize Jury, 1999:
'If any building can lift the spirits, this can.
A huge eye or screen looking down over
one of the most hallowed cricket grounds
in the world, the Media Centre is about
the idea that buildings can adopt, wholesale,
the construction methods developed by the
transport industries.

From the seamless exterior to the pale
blue interior inspired by a 1950s Chevrolet,
it's hard to imagine, even five years ago,
that this building would dominate Lord's
– and even more amazingly, those who use
it love it as much as we did.'

UNIQUE BUILDING: LORD'S MEDIA CENTRE
Jan Kaplicky/Future Systems – Stirling Prize winners, 1999

Winner of the last Stirling Prize of the 20th century, as well as seven other prestigious awards for design and construction, the NatWest Media Centre at Lord's received universal acclaim when it opened in April 1999. For once, critics were united in their praise of a structure which resulted from a ground-breaking collaboration between architects, engineers and boat-builders, producing the world's first semi-monocoque, all-aluminium, fully recyclable building.

With courage that belies their conservative image, the MCC had commissioned one of the most eye-catching and innovative buildings of recent times. Under the directorship of Jan Kaplicky, the London architectural firm Future Systems produced designs for the Media Centre in which structural techniques previously limited to the boat-building industry crossed the line into architecture. The smooth, curved aluminium structure – inspired by a combination of yacht structures, natural forms and the architects' sculptural sensitivities, but frequently compared to a spaceship or a friendly alien – appears to hover weightlessly over the cricket ground, dramatically cantilevered from two concrete piers which conceal its staircases and services. It can accommodate over 100 journalists, who enjoy an ideal view of the cricket ground through a vast glass front which is sharply angled to avoid any reflections or glare on the players. Every detail combines beauty with practicality: the icy mid-tone blues of the interior are used to minimise the contrast between the building's occupants and their background, and thus to avoid distraction if they move around during a match.

Unique Building is a comprehensive account of the commissioning, design and construction of this extraordinary building, which represents one of just a handful of built works from the many visionary, and often utopian, designs that Future Systems have produced. Along with a diverse array of photographs and sketches which express the form-finding mission that led to the final design, the book features all the working drawings and technical information, as well as a photographic 'diary' showing every stage of the cutting, welding and construction process. Unsurprisingly, there were many trials and tribulations along the way, as experts from previously unconnected fields attempted to reach understanding and agreement on the best ways to approach the task. The ups and downs of this creative process are documented in a series of revealing interviews with the key figures involved: boat-builder Henk Wiekens, engineer David Glover, MCC members Brian Thornton and Peter Bell, and the architects, Jan Kaplicky and Amanda Levete. These interviews offer compelling reading and, in conjunction with the outstanding visual material, make for a fascinating and stimulating book which includes everything there is to know about this distinctive building.

PB 0 471 98512 0, £24.95; 190 x 250 mm;
144 pages; January 2001

Subscribe Now for 2001

As an influential and prestigious architectural publication, *Architectural Design* has an almost unrivalled reputation worldwide. Published bi-monthly, it successfully combines the currency and topicality of a newsstand journal with the editorial rigour and design qualities of a book. Consistently at the forefront of cultural thought and design since the 60s, it has time and again proved provocative and inspirational – inspiring theoretical, creative and technological advances. Prominent in the 80s for the part it played in Post-Modernism and then in Deconstruction, ⚏ has recently taken a pioneering role in the technological revolution of the 90s. With ground-breaking titles dealing with cyberspace and hypersurface architecture, it has pursued the conceptual and critical implications of high-end computer software and virtual realities. ⚏

⚏ Architectural Design

SUBSCRIPTION RATES 2001
Institutional Rate: UK £150
Personal Rate: UK £97
Discount Student* Rate: UK £70
OUTSIDE UK
Institutional Rate: US $225
Personal Rate: US $145
Student* Rate: US $105

*Proof of studentship will be required when placing an order. Prices reflect rates for a 2001 subscription and are subject to change without notice.

UK/Europe: John Wiley & Sons Ltd.
Journals Administration Department
1 Oldlands Way
Bognor Regis
West Sussex PO22 9SA
UK

USA: John Wiley & Sons Ltd.
Journals Administration Department
605 Third Avenue
New York, NY 10158
USA

TO SUBSCRIBE

Phone your credit card order:
UK/Europe: +44 (0)1243 843 828
USA: +1 212 850 6645

Fax your credit card order to:
UK/Europe: +44 (0)1243 770 432
USA: +1 212 850 6021

Email your credit card order to:
cs-journals@wiley.co.uk

Post your credit card or cheque order to:

Please include your postal delivery address with your order.

All ⚏ volumes are available individually. To place an order please write to:
John Wiley & Sons Ltd
Customer Services
1 Oldlands Way
Bognor Regis
West Sussex PO22 9SA

Please quote the ISBN number of the issue(s) you are ordering.

⚏ is available to purchase on both a subscription basis and as individual volumes

---

○ I wish to subscribe to ⚏ Architectural Design at the **Institutional rate of £150**.

○ I wish to subscribe to ⚏ Architectural Design at the **Personal rate of £97**.

○ I wish to subscribe to ⚏ Architectural Design at the **Student rate of £70**.

STARTING FROM ISSUE 1/2001.

○ Payment enclosed by Cheque/Money order/Drafts.

Value/Currency £/US$ ☐

○ Please charge £/US$ ☐ to my credit card.

Account number:

☐☐☐☐☐☐☐☐☐☐☐☐☐☐☐☐☐

Expiry date:

☐☐☐☐☐☐

Card: Visa/Amex/Mastercard/Eurocard *(delete as applicable)*

Cardholder's signature ☐
Cardholder's name ☐
Address ☐
☐
☐ Post/Zip Code ☐

Recepient's name ☐
Address ☐
☐
☐ Post/Zip Code ☐

I would like to buy the following Back Issues at £19.99 each:

○ ⚏ 149 *Young Blood*, Neil Spiller

○ ⚏ 148 *Fashion and Architecture*, Martin Pawley

○ ⚏ 147 *The Tragic in Architecture*, Richard Patterson

○ ⚏ 146 *The Transformable House*, Jonathan Bell and Sally Godwin

○ ⚏ 145 *Contemporary Processes in Architecture*, Ali Rahim

○ ⚏ 144 *Space Architecture*, Dr Rachel Armstrong

○ ⚏ 143 *Architecture and Film II*, Bob Fear

○ ⚏ 142 *Millennium Architecture*, Maggie Toy and Charles Jencks

○ ⚏ 141 *Hypersurface Architecture II*, Stephen Perrella

○ ⚏ 140 *Architecture of the Borderlands*, Teddy Cruz

○ ⚏ 139 *Minimal Architecture II*, Maggie Toy

○ ⚏ 138 *Sci-Fi Architecture*, Maggie Toy

○ ⚏ 137 *Des-Res Architecture*, Maggie Toy

○ ⚏ 136 *Cyberspace Architecture II*, Neil Spiller

○ ⚏ 135 *Ephemeral/Portable Architecture*, Robert Kronenburg

○ ⚏ 134 *The Everyday and Architecture*, Sarah Wigglesworth

○ ⚏ 133 *Hypersurface Architecture*, Stephen Perrella

○ ⚏ 132 *Tracing Architecture*, Nikos Georgiadis

○ ⚏ 131 *Consuming Architecture*, Sarah Chaplin and Eric Holding